Orthodoxy in China

by Victor Selivanovsky and Eric S. Peterson

Translated from the Russian
by Olga V. Trubetskoy

SAINT IGNATIUS
ORTHODOX CHURCH
PRESS

Orthodoxy in China

Portions of this work previously appeared in materials
of the exhibit "Orthodoxy in China"
at the "Amurskaya Yarmarka," 2013
by the Missionary Department
of the Russian Orthodox Church,
Blagoveshchensk Diocese

With the blessings of His Grace Lukian, the Bishop of Blagoveshchensk and Tynda

Translated by Olga V. Trubetskoy

Editorial assistance: Lyubov Babkina, Vladimir S. Trubetskoy

Commentaries, footnotes and supplemental information: Eric S. Peterson

Chief editor of the English edition: Eric S. Peterson

ISBN10: 1508655618

ISBN-13:9781508655619

CONTENTS

ACKNOWLEDGMENTS

Even a small book is a large undertaking. This little book on the history of Orthodox Christianity in China, while it endeavors to bring together a wide array of information into one place, is by no means the last word on the subject. Let it serve as an introduction for those who have just heard that the Orthodox Church has been in China for centuries and continues to exist and grow, and may it be a catalyst for learning more about the missionary work of the Orthodox Church in China and throughout the world.

The translation of this book could not have been accomplished without, first and foremost, the grace of the Most Holy Trinity and the intercessions of the saints that the Orthodox Church of China has offered in great abundance, having been watered with the blood of martyrs and tended by the labors of ascetics and missionaries. To God and his saints and to the Orthodox Church at large we offer this work, the product of Orthodox Christians in Russia, China, and America.

We are grateful for the dedication and labor of Victor Selivanovsky, who wrote the Russian original, and Olga V. Trubetskoy, who translated it so that it could be read by an even wider audience. The "Orthodoxy in China" exhibits in Russia, in which materials from this book appeared, were also instrumental in bringing this good work to fruition. We would also like to thank Yin Hongbo, Lyubov Babkina and Vladimir S. Trubetskoy for their editorial assistance and Tatyana Pavlovich for her photographic materials.

We are grateful for the research of Father Denis Pozdnayev, missionary and scholar, and the labors of Mitrophan Chin, the webmaster of orthodox.cn, a treasure trove of information on Orthodoxy in China. Their work has allowed us to enrich the English translation with stories of the holy people and holy icons which have blessed the land of China with divine grace.

To His Grace Lukian, bishop of Blagoveshchensk and Tynda, who gave his blessing for this work, and to all the Orthodox clergy in China, Russia, and America who offered their blessings, prayers, scholarship, and encouragement, we wish to convey our gratitude, and pray that God preserve them for many years.

Finally, dear readers, we wish to thank you for your interest in the missions, history, and present life of the Chinese Orthodox Church.

FOREWORD

The Orthodox Church in China has existed for over three hundred years. Russians played an important role in establishing the Chinese Church (just as Greeks did in establishing Orthodox Christianity in Russia). The history of the Chinese Orthodox Church begins with the Russian Spiritual Mission in Peking (now Beijing). The mystical and sacred roots of the Church are in the blood of Chinese martyrs and in the feats of faith made by the forefathers of modern believers. This Church is alive! It is deeply rooted in several generations of Chinese who can claim that their grandparents and great-grandparents were Orthodox Christians. Today, the Orthodox Church in China is not large, and the Divine Liturgy is served only in a handful of active churches, but these very churches are now a focus of our prayers and intercessions.

1. THE BEGINNING OF THE ORTHODOX CHURCH IN CHINA

In the year 1685, Chinese imperial troops captured Fort Albazin, a Russian Far East outpost on the Amur River. It is worth noting that the guns used by the Manchurian troops were manufactured by Roman Catholic Jesuit missionaries. At that time, the Jesuits were already present in China for more than a hundred years and, together with the proclamation of the Gospel, they also brought Western technology to China [24, p. 166; 28, p.38].

During the battle, approximately fifty Cossacks from Fort Albazin (the Albazin Cossacks) were captured by the Chinese and sent to Peking (after 1911, the city's name is herein referred to as Beijing), where the Chinese later used them to form a military division of the Chinese Imperial Guard. The Albazin Cossacks were forced to settle in Peking in a special area by the northern part of the city walls called Bayguan, or the Northern Compound. They were also forced to change their Russian names to Chinese names and to take widows of executed Chinese criminals as their new wives.

Picture of Bayguan, where the Albazin Cossacks were settled.

An Orthodox priest, Father Maxim Leontiev, who was captured together with the Albazin Cossacks, built the first Orthodox church in China. For that purpose, he was allowed to remodel a pagan sanctuary originally dedicated to the pagan god of war, Guan-di [34, p.20]. The new Orthodox church was dedicated to the Holy Wisdom of God (Jesus Christ). The Albazin Cossacks sometimes also called it Nikol'skaya, or St. Nicholas Church, because of the very venerable icon of St. Nicholas the Wonderworker that was brought to China by the priest Maxim Leontiev.[1]

Sretenskaya Church (Church of the Presentation of Our Lord in the Temple), the oldest foreign building in Peking. It was destroyed in 1991.

---

[1] This icon was brought to the Soviet Union in 1956 by Archbishop Victor (Svyatin), the head of the last, 20th, Peking Orthodox Mission. [22, p.26]

4

Current photograph of the Uspenskaya (Assumption of the Theotokos) Church, built on the territory of the Orthodox Mission (now a part of the Russian consulate in China). The Uspenskaya Church was built in 1732, to replace the Holy Wisdom (Nikol'skaya) Church, the first Orthodox church in China, which was ruined by an earthquake in 1730. The Church of the Assumption was itself destroyed in 1900 by the members of the Boxer Rebellion movement,[2] and then restored in 1902. During the years of 1957-2008, the building was used as a garage by the Russian consulate. It was restored as an Orthodox church in 2009.

The story of what happened to the Albazin Cossacks was carried to the Russian Imperial Court in Saint Petersburg by caravans of travelling merchants. In 1700, Tsar Peter the Great issued an order about the caravan trade and the missionary activities of Orthodox priests in Siberia and the Tsin Empire (China). In this document, while discussing with the Russian Orthodox Patriarch of Moscow a possible candidate for Metropolitan of Tobolsk in Siberia, Peter the Great directed him to the following task:

"With the help of God, little by little, in China and in Siberia, to deliver knowledge and service and veneration of the true living God to the local

---

[2] The Boxer Rebellion, Boxer Uprising, or Yihetuan Movement was a proto-nationalistic movement in China from 1899-1901, which opposed foreign imperialism and Christian missions in China.

people who now are stiff and blind serving the idols and other false gods; and to bring to them two or three kind and learned, but not elderly monks, who upon learning the Chinese and Mongolian languages, writings, and the local pagan traditions, could, by the firm foundation of the Holy Gospel, bring many souls from evil darkness to the light of the knowledge of Christ, our God; and thus deliver local and coming Christians from the temptation to serve local idols; and thus they would live there and serve in God's church that they have built, so that by their good life they would bring the Chinese Khan and his close servants to this holy affair." [34, p.18]

Peter the Great saw the presence of the Albazin Cossacks in China as an opportunity for advancing Russian political and Orthodox spiritual goals. He approached the situation carefully, wary of drawing negative attention from either the Chinese government or representatives of other foreign powers. "This is a very important enterprise," he wrote. "But for God's sake, let us be cautious and circumspect, not to provoke either the Chinese authorities or the Jesuits, whose den is there since long ago. To this end, the clergymen are needed not so much as scholarly, but rather reasonable and amicable, lest this holy effort suffer a painful defeat because of a certain kind of arrogance" (V.P. Petrov. *Rossiskaya Dukhovnaya Missiia v Kitae*).

The death of the priest Maxim Leontiev in 1711 accelerated the necessity of sending the first Orthodox Spiritual Mission to China. The Mission was established in 1712, and included an archimandrite, a hieromonk, a hierodeacon and seven readers among its members.[3] In April of 1715, the Mission arrived in Peking.

The Russian Church was able to send the Mission because of the liberal policies of the Chinese Emperor Kangxi (1654-1722) of the Qing Dynasty. In 1692, Emperor Kangxi issued a manifesto proclaiming tolerance of Christianity and opened Chinese cities for trade with Europeans. The Mission also had some diplomatic functions, and the Chinese side was obliged to support the Mission materially.

The Russian Orthodox Church had plans to send Bishop Innocent (Kulchitsky, c. 1680-1731), to China with the second Mission (1729-1735),

---

[3] In the Orthodox Church, an archimandrite is a priest and monk who is given a higher degree of responsibility or honor than a hieromonk, who is simply a monk who has been ordained as a priest. A hierodeacon is a monk who is ordained as a deacon. Readers, in the Orthodox Church, are those men who receive an episcopal tonsure in order to chant and read the services in church, since Orthodox church services have many parts which are not performed by the priest or the congregation, such as the reading of Psalms.

but he was denied permission to enter China as a result of Jesuit intrigues and competition at the Chinese Imperial Court.

Unable to enter China, Bishop Innocent settled in the region of Lake Baikal and, following Tsar Peter's 1700 order on missionary activities, learned the local Mongolian languages and conducted missionary work among the indigenous peoples and the Russian population.

Now, **Saint Innocent of Irkutsk** (commemorated November 26/December 9) is venerated as a heavenly patron of China.

Canonical icon of St. Innocent (Kulchitsky), Bishop of Irkutsk (c. 1680-1731), one of the heavenly patrons of China.

The history of the Russian Orthodox Mission in China includes five major periods:

1. 1715-1858. This covers the period from the foundation of the Mission until the Treaty of Tianjin. After the agreement, the diplomatic functions of the spiritual mission ceased.

By the middle of the 19th century, there were around 200 Orthodox Christians in Peking (Hattaway, Paul. China's Book of Martyrs (AD 845-present), p. 291). The Albazinians, the Chinese descendants of the original Cossack captives, helped to train interpreters for Russo-Chinese diplomatic relations (Latourette, Kenneth Scott. A History of Christian Missions in China, p. 486).

2. 1858-1900. During this time, Chinese central authority was substantially weakened through a succession of wars with foreign powers (such as the Opium Wars) and domestic rebellions. Foreign powers demanded and received concessions from the Chinese government to operate Christian missions throughout China. (Prior to this time, Christian

missionaries and Chinese Christian converts were sometimes persecuted by the state.)

Several of the domestic rebellions also had religious dimensions, such as the Taiping Rebellion (1851-1864), which was begun by a Chinese man, Hong Xiuquan, who, upon suffering a nervous breakdown with an extended fever and having a series of dreams, began a religious movement claiming to be the younger brother of Jesus Christ and a divine messiah. He had earlier received Christian missionary materials and even studied with an American Southern Baptist missionary.

At that time, many Protestant missionaries in China favored an evangelization strategy whereby they would blanket whole areas with tracts, often leaving those who received the tracts to interpret them according to their own way of thinking. Typically, the tracts would include instructions, such as how to be baptized. Hong and his cousin were baptized according to instructions in the pamphlet, "Good Words to Admonish the Age" (Franz, Michael. The Taiping Rebellion: History and Documents, Volume One, pg. 25).

By 1850, Hong had gained between 10,000 and 30,000 followers, mainly peasants. He and his followers would lead raids on Confucian and Buddhist sites and destroy the religious statuary. The movement was also anti-Manchu. The Manchus were a non-Chinese ethnic group, hailing from Manchuria, who had ruled China in the Qing Dynasty since 1644, and had forced the majority Han Chinese to adopt Manchu dress and hairstyles. The Taiping Rebellion provoked one of the largest military operations in history, in terms of troop involvement. In order to crush the rebellion, the Qing government received assistance from French and British troops. An estimated 20 million people were killed in the decade-long war to end the rebellion.

Later rebellions would capitalize on escalating anti-Qing and anti-foreign sentiments. Christian missionaries and Chinese Christian converts were persecuted or tolerated, depending on the prevailing political conditions and public opinion.

The Boxer Rebellion (1899-1901), referred to in Chinese as the "Brigades of Righteous and Harmonious Fists," distinguished itself from previous rebellions in that it maintained a pro-Qing stance. Its slogan was "Support the Qing, exterminate the foreigners." The movement came to be known for particularly savage bouts of violence, resulting in the massacres of over 200 Chinese Orthodox Christians and thousands of Roman Catholic and Protestant Christians, both foreign missionaries and

Chinese converts throughout China. It was a reaction against the consequences of foreign influence and unequal treaties that infringed on Chinese sovereignty. Initially, the Boxers had support from the Chinese Empress Cixi and other Qing officials, but the government later changed course and the Boxer Rebellion, like the Taiping, was crushed with the aid of foreign powers.

Perceived threats from foreign influence would shape Chinese government policy regarding Christian missionary work from the 19th century to the present day.

The relatively small size of the Orthodox Mission in China, in comparison to the Roman Catholic and Protestant missions, warrants explanation lest unfair conclusions be drawn. The Protestant and Roman Catholic missionaries received funding from the many countries from which their missionaries came—Protestants from Great Britain, the United States, and Australia; Roman Catholics from France, Italy, and the Austro-Hungarian Empire—to name only a few. Both had powerful lobbies at home, with strong political connections and capable fundraising organizations. Their missionaries also received military backing and protection from their governments, and these governments, in turn, worked to win concessions from the Chinese to further Roman Catholic and Protestant missionary efforts.

In contrast, the Orthodox Mission in China received little financial support from the Russian government. The Russian diplomatic and trade presence in China was considerably smaller than that of other powers. Russia's sphere of influence was largely centered in Central Asia and Manchuria, near the Russian Far East, rather than in the large port cities of the south where Western nations had their power bases. The Orthodox missions were located mainly in northern and central China. All of these factors, and the unique character of the Albazinians as an isolated indigenous Sino-Russian community in Peking for the first 200 years of its existence, contributed to the relatively small size of the Orthodox presence in China.

Yet, despite these circumstances, the Orthodox Mission did experience large growth. A number of Chinese converted to Orthodoxy when daily services in Mandarin began in 1897 (Hattaway, p. 291). By 1900, there were Orthodox churches not only in Peking, but in the provinces (ibid).

3. 1900-1917. This period saw a rapid rise in missionary activities all over China, including the opening of new schools and churches, and growth in Christian missionary and charities. Despite the destruction wreaked by the

9

Boxer Rebellion, by the end of 1914 there were 32 Orthodox Christian mission centers in the provinces of Hebei, Hubei, Henan, Jiangsu and Inner Mongolia (ibid, p. 292). These missions "enrolled 500 pupils in [their] schools, and claimed a Chinese baptized membership of 5,035" (Latourette, pgs. 583-84, citing figures from the China Mission Year Book, 1915).

Today, there are still descendants of the Albazin Cossacks living in Beijing, and most remain Orthodox believers (Hattaway, p. 292).

4. 1917-1945. This period saw a great influx of Russian immigrants into China after the Russian Revolution. The Chinese Orthodox Mission adapted to help these immigrants.

5. 1945-1956. In this period, the Chinese Orthodox Church came under the administration of the Moscow Patriarchate. (In the previous period, it had been administered primarily by the Russian Orthodox Church Abroad.) This period saw a renewal of missionary work to the native Chinese population and attempts to organize what would later become, in 1956, the autonomous Orthodox Church of China.

During the last 250 years, there have been 20 Chinese Orthodox Spiritual Missions altogether. Each mission spent, on average, 10 years in China. The last mission was closed in 1956, and all its assets were transferred to the government officials of the People's Republic of China.

The autonomous Orthodox Church of China became the spiritual successor of the Orthodox Spiritual Mission. However, the complete organization of the autonomous Orthodox Church of China in the 1950s was not formalized. The following years, and especially the years of the Chinese "Cultural Revolution" from 1966-1976, when churches were destroyed and priests were murdered, were years of terrible suffering for the Chinese Church. With the deaths of so many priests, the Church hierarchy was destroyed.

2. PREACHING THE GOSPEL

Cultural Adaptation

In terms of dress rules, common rituals, and specific domestic issues, each missionary should adapt to the culture and environment where he preaches. For example, the priest Maxim Leontiev, the first Orthodox priest in China, who was captured together with Albazin Cossacks, "during the war between the Chinese and the Kalmyk, when he followed the Cossacks in their military action, had his hair cut in the Manchurian style" [28, p.56]. Similarly, Mateo Ricci, the first Jesuit missionary in China at the end of the 16th century, used to dress in the style of a Chinese Confucian scholar.

Such methods are called acculturation or adaptation to an indigenous culture. However, each missionary also faces another very important task, namely, how to determine the acceptable boundaries of adaptation to the pagan culture.

From that point of view, one of the most problematic issues among Chinese cultural phenomena is the cult of ancestor veneration. This cult has a centuries-long tradition in China and includes rituals such as venerating tablets inscribed with the names of deceased ancestors, sacrificial acts, and the burning of paper "spirit money" (not real money, but symbolic), with the goal of honoring one's ancestors, ensuring their happiness in the afterlife, and entreating their help and protection.

There are three fundamental beliefs underlying ancestor veneration: 1. that one's ancestors continue to exist after death, 2. that the familial bond between a person and his or her ancestors also continues after death, and 3. that the ancestors possess greater spiritual power in the afterlife than they did prior to death, and thus have the ability to interact with and affect the lives of those who are still living (Thompson, L.G. Chinese Religion: An Introduction, Third Edition, 1979).

In these fundamentals, there is a strong similarity to Orthodox Christian teaching with regard to the eternal life of the soul, the resurrection of the dead, prayers for the dead, and the intercession of the saints. Despite these similarities, however, there is a distinctly pagan (and not simply Confucian) metaphysics underlying traditional Chinese ancestor veneration, particularly with regard to beliefs and rituals associated with the cult.

The very thin boundary in the Confucian school of thought defining a difference between respect and veneration of the ancestors is not very clear. Confucius himself was never definite when answering a direct question about the ancestors' afterlife and the meaning of sacrificial rituals relating to the ancestor cult: "When asked about the meaning of bringing sacrificial food to the ancestors, and if the deceased could eat such food, Confucius answered: "Not by any means, but we should do it for the purpose of developing a respect for our ancestors, like if they were alive." [21, p.131]. The Russian Orthodox Mission was tolerant to Confucius and the veneration of the tablets with names as perceived from the ethical perspective only, but condemned the sacrificial gifts and "afterlife money."

In such situations, the Orthodox missionaries followed the "liberal" traditions of the Jesuits that were established by Matteo Ricci in the 17th century.

However, at the beginning of the 18th century, a very heated debate on this issue was started by the different orders of the Roman Catholic Church. The most radical position was held by the members of the Franciscan and Dominican Orders, who considered all elements of the cult to be a part of pagan tradition.

Therefore, newly converted Christians in China were in a very difficult position because the complete denial of the tradition of ancestor veneration meant for them a complete loss of their national identity. When the Vatican condemned the veneration of Confucius and the ancestral name tablets, it led to a closure of the Catholic mission in China for 120 years, from 1724 till 1844. This decree was annulled by the Vatican only at the beginning of 1930s, during the Japanese occupation of China.

The Japanese occupiers in China required everyone's participation in civil ceremonies, including bowing to Confucius, bowing to the site of the residence of the Japanese Emperor, and also bowing to the site of the temple of the sun goddess Amateras as a symbol of the Japanese Empire [13, p.15]. Refusal to participate in such rituals led to severe punishment.

The Russian Orthodox parishes in China had many members at that time and they all accepted the bowing towards the country of the Rising Sun as a civil ceremony, but refused to accept the "Directives to the Submissive Citizens" issued by the occupiers in 1942. The first point of the Directives stated that "all submissive citizens of the Empire of Manchou-go[4] have to reverently venerate the goddess Amateras." Though the Japanese occupiers later nullified these Directives, there were known cases where Orthodox Christians were imprisoned and Orthodox priests were exiled for their refusal to follow them.

Theological Adaptation

In 1810, the head of the 9th Spiritual Mission, Fr. Ioakinf (Bichurin) published an Orthodox catechism in the Chinese language called "Conversations among the Angels" [34, p.46], based on the Jesuit Chinese catechism of 1730. Confessional differences between Roman Catholics and Orthodox in China turned out to be less important compared to the main missionary task – to proclaim the personal God, an idea that hardly existed in Chinese religious tradition. In the 16th century, the Jesuit Matteo Ricci came out with a method of theological adaptation seeking "to enrich the Confucian theology, but to reject Buddhism." Such methods were also adapted by the Orthodox missionaries [24, p.3].

From the many religious elements of China, only an early Confucian platform, from before the neo-Confucian reform of the 11th century, was suitable for the Orthodox missionaries. "Confucius never spoke about gods, but he talked about Heaven" [36, p.50]. "I can't stop thinking about Confucius as the theist. His childlike relationship with Heaven, that for him meant another name for God, was the source of his greatness," wrote Prof. U. Tsinsuin, a Chinese ambassador to the Vatican [40, pp58-59].

For the missionaries, it was possible to reduce early Confucianism to monotheism, but not Buddhism, due to its denial of the God-Creator. However, some other elements of Buddhism were very relevant to Christianity, since they recognized the life after death, heaven and hell. One of the main difficulties for the missionaries was presented by the special characteristics of the Chinese mentality, which considered human nature as

---

[4] Manchou-go was a marionette state, existing from 1932-1944, created by the Japanese occupiers with the last Chinese Emperor as a head of state.

self-sufficient, with no understanding for the need of the atoning sacrifice of Christ. The Christian understanding of the idea of sin and a fallen human nature is unique among many religions.

As for preaching an idea of the crucified Christ, that was difficult to accept even in pagan Hellenistic tradition because it looked like madness to them (see 1 Cor. 1:23). Therefore, the Christian missionaries in China did not put an accent of the Passion of Christ, but rather concentrated on his Resurrection and Ascension.

Gospel Preaching after the Treaties of Tianjin and Aigun

The Treaty of Tianjin[5] signed in 1858 allowed Christian missionaries to return to China. From the Russian side, the agreement was signed by Count E.V. Poutiatin, who warned about the necessity of growing an Orthodox preaching among the other Christian confessions in China. Since 1863, the diplomatic functions of the Orthodox Mission had ceased, and another opportunity to send an Orthodox bishop to China arrived. However, despite that, the Mission budget was slashed in half, not allowing funds for an Orthodox bishop to have a cathedra (administrative center). There were serious discussions in the Russian State Assembly (*Gosudarstvennii Soviet*) regarding setting up an Orthodox bishopric in China, but it was never accomplished at that time since it required increased representation and financing for the Mission, with an annual budget of up to 14,560 rubles. Instead, the Mission funding was reduced from 17,750 to 8,875 rubles per annum [18, p285]. At that moment, a strict subordination of the Church to the State led to the most negative consequences for the whole history of the Mission.

---

[5] The Treaty of Tianjin (Tien-tsin), signed in June of 1858, ended the first part of the Second Opium War (1856-1860). The Russian Empire was among the signatories, along with Great Britain, France, and the United States. The treaty opened Chinese ports, set up foreign embassies in Peking (prior to that time, it was a city closed to foreigners), allowed for Christian missionary activity in China, and legalized opium imports into China. (In the 17th century, the practice of mixing opium with tobacco for smoking was introduced into China by Europeans. British traders held a virtual monopoly on opium imports into China. A significant outflow of silver, together with a surge in opium addiction, caused the Chinese government to suppress the opium trade. In response, the British sent military forces to China and forced the Chinese government to capitulate and allow for an expansion of the opium trade, together with granting foreign citizens extraterritorial rights, and the ceding of territory, including Hong Kong, to Great Britain. As a result of the Opium Wars, China lost much of its sovereignty and came to be viewed by the Western powers as a rich export market for Western goods and ideas, attracting hundreds of traders and missionaries from around the world. In China, however, the Opium Wars began what is called the "Century of Humiliation," and xenophobic feelings increased with each new display of Western power

However, in 1861, the Orthodox Mission in China made its first expansion outside of Peking. An Orthodox school was opened in the village of Doudinyan, where ten families in the village were of Russian descent [24, p.314]. During this time, the Mission was actively involved in the translation of the Orthodox liturgical texts into Chinese. However, the true territorial expansion of the Mission began only after 1900.

Preaching in the Far East

The Amur River region became a part of the Russian Empire after Russia signed the Treaty of Aigun[6] with China in 1858. At this time, the Amur region also became a part of the Kamchatka Diocese of the Russian Orthodox Church. From 1840 until 1868, the head of the Kamchatka Diocese was Bishop **Innocent (Veniaminov, 1797-1879, commemorated March 31/April 13 and Sept. 23/Oct. 6)**, who later became the Metropolitan of Moscow. [7]

After 30 years of missionary work among Aleuts, Koloshi, and Yakuts, St. Innocent wanted to "send missionaries to Manchuria, as soon as possible and as far as possible" [27, p223]. For that purpose, he worked out several practical measures.

---

and influence over China. Later, especially in the Boxer Rebellion, Christians would be seen as a symbol of Western domination and Chinese humiliation, and would suffer for it.

[6] The Treaty of Aigun, signed in 1858, set the border between the Russian and Chinese Empires, particularly with regard to the Russian Far East and Chinese Manchuria.

[7] St. Innocent Veniaminov (1797-1879), born John Popov in the Irkutsk Province, served as a missionary priest and later a bishop in the Aleutian Islands, Alaska, Kamchatka, and in the Yakutsk and Amur Regions before becoming Metropolitan of Moscow. In each region he learned the local language, translating Church texts and even writing original works, creating some of the first literature for those indigenous languages. He also made extensive ethnographic notes on the indigenous peoples he evangelized. In his instructions to missionaries, he stressed character (prayer, humility, self-control, thoughtfulness, and love), never missing an opportunity to teach, leniency and understanding with regard to indigenous customs insomuch as they may conflict with Christian norms (such as fasting, which the Orthodox do by eliminating animal products from their diet in certain seasons— indigenous Siberians and Alaskans, being primarily nomadic hunters, obtain a majority of their calories from animal products). He opposed any coercive measures, whether bribes or threats, in order to make converts, and ordered that no baptisms be performed without thorough instruction in the Orthodox faith. Missionaries were not to present themselves as government officials or to meddle in temporal affairs, but rather to present themselves as ones wishing goodwill to their fellow men. On no account were missionaries to show contempt for the natives' way of life, but instead they were to learn their language, culture, and religious beliefs and practices. He forbade them from requiring presents or funds from the natives, and from entering into commercial transactions with them. His instructions to missionaries are still referenced today in handbooks for contemporary Orthodox missionaries.

Portrait of St. Innocent (Veniaminov, 1797-1879), the Metropolitan of Moscow (left) and canonical icon of St. Innocent of Moscow.

First, he asked to transfer Hieromonk Evlampiy (Ivanov) from the Peking mission to Blagoveshchensk (the capital of the Amur region). Evlampiy had knowledge of the Chinese and Manchurian languages, but he died soon after arriving in Blagoveshchensk in 1863, before starting his work with St. Innocent. Since no other Orthodox missionaries were available in China, St. Innocent decided to start preparing his own missionary forces. In 1864, the Blagoveshchensk Diocesan School started Manchurian language classes. Also a Manchurian Mission was initiated, but there were no missionaries until 1868, the year of St. Innocent's departure from the Far East to Moscow.

Roman Tsyrenpilov, a priest of the Kamchatka Diocese, became the first missionary on the right (Manchurian) bank of the Amur River. He was an ethnic Buryat and quickly learned the Manchurian language. For three years, he visited Manchurian villages from Sakhalyan (Heyhe) to Hormoldzin, preaching the Gospel and giving away Manchurian translations of the New Testament. According to him, "the words of the Gospel have become the living faith of many who have read it." However, only one young Manchurian man was actually baptized as an Orthodox Christian. At the same time, the Gospel preaching to the Manchurians on the Russian bank of the Amur River was more successful. According to the census of 1897, there were 38 Chinese and eight Manchurian Orthodox

Christians in the Amur region, and 85 in the Far East region, even in the absence of the official Mission [27, p. 238, 240].

Chinese merchants and service providers from the boundary regions involved in cultural exchanges with Russians were the ones most interested in Orthodoxy. Many of them came to discussions at the Amba-Lama's (archpriest's) house where the bishop of Blagoveshchensk lived and a temporary missionary station was organized. In 1893, Trifontai, one of the wealthiest Chinese merchants in the Amur region, was baptized and "many other merchants wanted to follow his example" [27, p.236]. In 1895, a Chinese woman named Alatu came all the way from central China to Blagoveshchensk to be baptized, and was baptized as Yekaterina. Altogether,
350 Chinese and 15 Manchurians were baptized as Orthodox Christians from 1864 to 1915 in the Far East region [27, p.242].

The process of Christianizing the Chinese met with serious socio-political difficulties since Chinese authorities issued repressive laws against Chinese citizens baptized as Christians. Bishop Benjamin, who succeeded St. Innocent Veniaminov to the throne of the Kamchatka Diocese,[8] wrote: "As for the Russian (Orthodox) faith, acceptance of it, in the eyes of local Chinese authorities, is equivalent the acceptance of Russian citizenship" [35, p.54].
A Chinese neophyte merchant baptized as an Orthodox Christian would immediately lose his part in the financial capital of his firm. At that time, most Chinese merchant firms were collective proprietorships, with between ten and forty members. If a merchant required his capital, even before becoming a Christian, with such a request he had to travel from Manchuria to China, to the central office of the company. Hieromonk Stephan, a missionary for the Kamchatka Diocese with close relations to Chinese merchants, wrote in 1894: "But there, betrayed by his companions, he would never get his capital, but instead, for the acceptance of the Orthodox faith or even for the consideration of the acceptance, he would lose his life through beheading" [19, p.195].

Neophyte laborers faced even more challenges. Chinese workers were hostile to them, but even Russian labor groups of bricklayers or carpenters did not accept Chinese workers. As a result, such people became outcasts, rejected by the society, unable to work and feed themselves. Though an Orthodox Brotherhood in Blagoveshchensk helped them, such help was not sufficient.

---

[8] The Blagoveshchensk cathedra since 1899.

On top of that, there was the hostility of the Buddhist lamas to the overall activities of Christian missionaries and, above all, the short-sighted policies of the Russian authorities. One such policy, issued in 1888 by Baron A.V. Korf, governor-general of the Amur region, was a demand to cut the traditional Chinese braid after baptism into Orthodoxy. This was a serious matter since the Qing Dynasty, as a matter of law, required the braid to be worn by all Chinese citizens. On this issue, Hieromonk Stephan wrote: "For us missionaries, there is no use baptizing those Chinese, who are not Russian citizens, since by returning to China without their traditional braid, they will be either killed or forced to reject Christianity"[20, p.527].

Because of these problems, Chinese who were inquiring about an Orthodox baptism in the Russian Far East often asked to become Russian citizens also. Therefore, as a result of political and cultural issues, in the second half of 19th century, religious identification was often closely associated with national identity. Such conditions prevailed until the beginning of the 20th century.

By contrast, the Orthodox Albazinians in Peking, prior to the Treaty of Tianjin, were in the enviable position of living in the Forbidden City, close to the emperor, and enjoyed a modicum of imperial protection. Such protection and respect, however, did not extend outside of Peking or to non- Albazinians.[9]

The situation for Chinese Orthodox and Non-Orthodox Christian converts throughout China changed after the suppression of the Boxer Rebellion, leading to an escalation in the number of Chinese converting to Christianity. The Xinhai Revolution[10] of 1911, and events that followed, created favorable conditions for the Christianization of China. Metropolitan Innocent (Figurovsky) wrote about these issues: "The revolutionary movement that crushed the deification of the Imperial power in China, has shaken all paganism to its foundations. Leaving behind all the moribund tradition of ancestors, Chinese people started to listen more attentively to the apostolic sermons of the Christian churches of all confessions. A number of Christians in the new government are now sympathetic to the Gospel.

---

[9] Eric Widmer, "The Russian Ecclesiastical Mission in Peking During the Eighteenth Century" (Harvard East Asian Monographs).

[10] The Xinhai Revolution, or the Hsin-hai Revolution, also known as the Revolution of 1911 or the Chinese Revolution, overthrew China's last imperial dynasty, the Qing, and established the Republic of China.

preaching..."[27, p.245-246]. Such observations were later confirmed by the fact that one of China's leaders, Chiang Kai-shek, became a Christian in the Methodist denomination in 1930.

Chinese Christians today fully accept themselves as Chinese and do not experience problems with self-identification. The modern history of China has changed the socio-cultural landscape of the country and transformed the people's social consciousness. At the same time, the atheistic ideology and nihilistic propaganda against the country's cultural heritage during the "Cultural Revolution," from 1966-76, further undermined the pagan traditions of the society. The latter also changed the tone and characteristics of missionary sermons. Father Dmitry Pozdnyaev, a modern Orthodox missionary in Hong Kong, writes that "in a modern secular China, an apologetic approach to Christianity based on Confucius will likely not find real support in the hearts and minds of our contemporaries. Indeed, the most likely approach to the modern intellectual elite in China would be a sermon on Christianity using the language of modern science and philosophy. The majority of people in this great country, where 70 percent of citizens are still peasants, await a preaching about Christ in a simple manner, towards simple hearts; not a preaching immersed in books, but a preaching full of evangelical good news and hope for salvation. A clear and understandable testimony of Orthodoxy, Orthodox spiritual practice, and theology is the best way of preaching in modern China."

3. TRANSLATIONS OF THE BIBLE

The first translation of the New Testament into Chinese was done in 1707 by the French Roman Catholic Jean Basset. He used the Latin Vulgate Bible, which dates from the fourth century and is the official text of the Roman Catholic Church.

In 1822, S.V. Lipovtsev, a member of 8th Spiritual Mission to China, accomplished a translation of the New Testament into the Manchurian language [28, p.25, p.28, p.228]. This translation was first published in St. Petersburg in 1826, and was later reprinted by the London Missionary Society. By that time, two Protestant translations of Bible existed, the most well-known being the Morrison-Miln translation of 1823 [24, p.254-255].

In 1864, the Russian Spiritual Mission printed the first Chinese translation of the New Testament made by Archimandrite, later Archbishop Gury Karpov.[11] The translation was based on the works of previous Missions, though "the language of translation was too educated" [1, p.121]. Another translation of the New Testament was done by Archimandrite Flavian (Gorodetsky) and published in 1889. Archimandrite Flavian

---

[11] **St. Gury (Karpov, 1812-1882, commemorated on March 17/30)** was head of the 14th Spiritual Mission in China (1858-1864). He was glorified as a saint by the Ukrainian Orthodox Church (Moscow Patriarchate) on August 23, 2008. He was an erudite scholar of Orthodox theology and the Chinese language. Besides the New Testament, St. Gury translated several other works into Chinese, including: "Four Principles of Spiritual Cultivation," a catechism, the Church lectionary, several Church prayers, and the lives of many saints. His feast day is March 17, the day of his repose in the Lord. His holy relics are incorrupt.

reworked the "previous translation of the Gospel texts and published it again ... with footnotes giving explanations" [6, p.201]. At the beginning of the 20th century, Chinese Orthodox Christians had three of their own Chinese translations of the New Testament, done by the work of the Mission.

"Protestant churches several times have made reprints of the translations made by former heads of our Mission, Blessed Gury and Flavian," wrote the Mission historian Hieromonk Nikolai (Adoratsky) [1, p.123].

A photograph of Archbishop Gury and canonical icon of St. Gury (Karpov, 1812-1882), the head of 14th Spiritual Mission.

In 1910, yet another Chinese translation of the New Testament by Metropolitan Innocent (Figurovsky) was published [34, p.108]. This text was very close to the modern spoken language, though it still contained prepositions and grammar fragments from classical Chinese [17]. A common defect of the 19th century translations was that they used archaic, classical Chinese, and therefore, were not accessible for many. Already at the beginning of the 20th century, missionaries preferred making translations into vernacular Chinese, as opposed to the classical literary form, which was not widely understood.

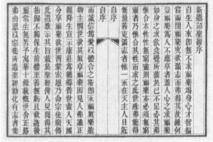

New Testament printed by the Russian Spiritual Mission in China, Peking, 1910 (left). Translation of the New Testament by Archimandrite, later Archbishop Gury (Karpov), published by the Russian Spiritual Mission in China, 1864 (right).

These past translations of the Russian Spiritual Mission are now obsolete. Today's Orthodox missionaries prefer to use Roman Catholic translations of the Bible into contemporary Chinese.

The Names of God

The missionary-translators of the Bible had the task of explaining the idea of a personal God using concepts previously known to the Chinese, but at the same time avoiding pagan connotations.

Some of the earliest Christian missionaries to arrive in China, Persians from the Church of the East (often, and mistakenly before 780 AD, called Nestorian, with their patriarch located in Seleucia-Ctesiphon in modern-day Iraq) brought Christianity to China in around 635 AD. The Christian faith in Chinese was called Jǐng jiào (景教, literally, 'bright teaching'). The Persian missionaries' Chinese term for God was Zhēnzhǔ (真主, literally

22

'Veritable Majesty,' or 'True Lord.'[12] This name for God appears to have been original, but the term Zhenzhu was employed as a regnal name of the second Khan of Xueyantuo, a kingdom once located in the area of the Selenga River, south of Lake Baikal, in Greater Mongolia. This khan died in 645 AD.

The Church of the East mission was located farther to the south in the Tang Dynasty capital of Chang'an, in China proper, but one might make the inference that their term for God, "Zhenzhu," while not inspired by the Xueyantuo khan, was at least a title of contemporary understanding to the Chinese.

Later Christian missionaries would delve further into Chinese cultural history to find the right term for God[13] in Chinese such as:

天主 (Tianzhu), or "Heavenly Lord" – This name most adequately reflects the theological novelty of Christianity, but is absent in the Chinese classical system of thought.

上帝 (Shangdi), or "Above Emperor" – This name exists in Taoist literature.[14] The Chinese consciousness may also refer to Shangdi as to the "anonymous life giving force of the Universe" [24, p.97, 175].

The Roman Catholic Jesuit missionary Matteo Ricci in the 17th century allowed both versions. However, at the beginning of the 18th century, the dispute among the different Roman Catholic religious orders also involved the names of God. The Vatican confirmed the name "Heavenly Lord" (Tianzhujiao), whereas Protestants in the 19th century preferred the name "Above Emperor" (Shangdi).

Orthodox translations of the 19th century used "Tianzhujiao,"

---

[12] http://en.wikipedia.org/wiki/Chinese_terms_for_God

[13] In recent years, some Protestants have adopted the term Shén, or 神, for God. However, this term is quite generic. It can mean a god or God, but also a spirit or a soul. By using "Shen," these Protestants hoped to avoid the cultural connotations of "Shangdi" and "Tianzhujiao," but instead have to reckon with the theological imprecision of a term which could mean either the uncreated God, or a created spirit or soul.

[14] The "Tao," in Chinese thought, is often translated as the "Way," but Christian translators of Scripture used "Tao" to translate the Greek term "Logos" into Chinese, so that the beginning of the Gospel of St. John reads, when translated from Chinese into English, "In the beginning was the Tao, and the Tao was with God, and the Tao was God." This hearkens to the verse later in the same Gospel, where the Lord Jesus Christ says, "I am the Way, the Truth, and the Life" (John 14:6). Just as the early Holy Fathers built on the ancient, pre-Christian Greek philosophical concept of the Logos, so the Christian missionaries used the ancient Chinese concept of the Tao to illustrate the meaning of the Christian message.

23

whereas, from the beginning of the 20th century, they started using "Shangdi."

道 – Tao (Dào) = Logos. While writing his Gospel, St. John the Theologian used the Greek term "Logos," which existed already in early Greek pre-Christian philosophy. "Logos" was translated into English as "Word." However, in Greek tradition this term is more complex and could have about 30 different meanings. It could mean an existing order in nature, a general model of the universe, or a rational foundation of some subjects, e.g. logic as a part of many branches of science.

The Apostle John wrote that the Logos was the Word of God, the second hypostasis (or person) of the Holy Trinity (the Father, the Son, and the Holy Spirit), and that the Word, or Logos, or Tao of God became man in Jesus Christ.

Such an example allowed translators to use the term "Tao" from Chinese philosophy, similar in its meaning to the Greek "Logos."

The modern standard Chinese translation the Gospel of St. John starts as follows:
"最初它是道，道在上帝那里，道就是上帝。" – "At the beginning it was Tao, and Tao was at Shangdi, and Tao was Shangdi." [15]

The translators from the Russian Spiritual Mission attempted to preserve the historical connection of Chinese Albazinians with Russian liturgical tradition. Therefore, when transcribing the name of Jesus Christ, they used the characters which would be phonetically similar to Slavic pronunciation. They chose the variant "Yesusi Helisytosi," though at that time missionaries of other confessions were using the term "Yesu Tsidu" [134, p.72]. Phonetic similarity to Slavic pronunciation was preserved also in the translation of geographical names in the Bible and in other terms such as "alleluia," "hosanna," "Pascha," "pharaoh," "cherubim," and "seraphim."

---

[15] A more common variant is: "At the beginning it was Tao, Tao was one with the Spirit, Tao which is the Spirit." (This particular modern translation uses "Shen" or "Spirit" to refer to God, rather than "Shangdi," or "Above Emperor."

Chinese Liturgy

In 1883 - 1884, the Russian Spiritual Mission finished Chinese translations of most liturgical texts used by the Orthodox Church, such as the Liturgy of St. John Chrysostom and the Sunday Octoechos.[16] That allowed for starting church services in Chinese.

The head of 16th Mission, Archimandrite Flavian (Gorodetsky), was the one who first started the practice of praying the divine services in Chinese [34, p. 82]. "Thanks to the pedal organ (or harmonium) purchased by the Mission, it became possible to organize a church choir of more than 20 members. Starting in 1883, this choir harmoniously sang from two sides – on the right in Church Slavonic, on the left in Chinese [17] [1, p.122].

The liturgical and service texts of the Mission were later sent to Japan where they were translated into Japanese and became a part of the service texts of the Japanese Orthodox Church. Saint Nicholas (Kasatkin) of Japan wrote the following about it: "The Mission in Peking is the mother of the Japanese [Mission]. Without Peking, the Japanese are inexperienced and have no voice [that is, speechless, unable to pray in their own language]" [1, p.122].

The first Chinese Orthodox priest, Father Mitrofan Tzi, started church services in his native language in 1882. In contrast, the Roman Catholic Church allowed services in native languages only after the Second Vatican Council in 1964.

---

[16] This edition was published in 20 volumes [28, p.25]. At that time, the entire volume of translation consisted of 300,000 Chinese characters [34, p.82]. The Octoechos is a service book of the Orthodox Church which includes hymns for the daily cycle of services, following eight tones or musical styles.

[17] According to Chinese tradition, the left side is more honorable.

Divine Liturgy for Albazinians in the Peking Cathedral in 1857.
A drawing scene from life by an artist I.I. Chmutov, a member of 13th Mission.

4. CHINESE MARTYRS

In modern Chinese historiography, the Boxer Rebellion in China, also called the *I-ho ch'uan* or *Yihetuan* Movement of 1900, is called an anti-imperialistic uprising. Therefore, in a given political context, "those who suffered during the uprising are said to have suffered for a 'just cause'"[31].[18]

The underlying reasons for the Boxer Rebellion were complex— including missionaries' negative stances toward the pagan foundations of Chinese culture, governmental officials' envy of the missionaries' privileges, a bad harvest, unemployment as a result of the incorporation of Western industrial technologies, and resentment of Chinese dependence on the West.

However, the Boxer Rebellion movement had a primarily religious character. The rebels called themselves Buddhists, and they referred to their targets—Christians, foreigners and Chinese alike—as "devils." The Boxers,
with the help and collusion of the Chinese authorities, killed tens of thousands of foreign Christian missionaries and Chinese Christians. Among them were 222 Chinese Orthodox Christians—including men, women, and children—whom the Orthodox Church has canonized as martyrs for the faith. (For more information on the Chinese Orthodox Martyrs of the Boxer Rebellion, see Appendix IV.)

The memory of these Chinese martyrs is celebrated on June 11/24 after their canonization in 1902 [12, p.29].

---

[18] Communist political propaganda justifies all anti-imperialistic movements of the past as fights for a "just cause" and all their victims as "those who suffered justly."

An icon of the Assembly (Synaxis) of the Holy Chinese Martyrs, at the Russian Orthodox Cathedral in San Francisco named after the icon of the Mother of God "Joy of all Who Sorrow."[19]

---

[19] In the year 2000, the Roman Catholic Church canonized 120 Chinese Roman Catholics as victims of the Boxer Rebellion, which led to a diplomatic conflict with China.

The rebellion movement started in the province of Shan'dun, the birthplace of Confucius. The location had great spiritual significance for the uprising. Boxer proclamations mentioned the following: "Today, the skies are angry with Jesus' teachings because it insults spirits, annihilates sacred Confucius' instructions, and does not respect Buddhism. Therefore, the skies are withholding rain and sending 8,000,000 heavenly warriors to destroy the foreigners" [4, p.35].

Mysticism played a significant role in the rebellion. For example, the Boxers claimed to see columns of white smoke above the roofs of the Christian "devils."

Chinese government officials were uncertain in their position—whether to support or suppress the rebels—however, xenophobic dispositions were prevalent in the Chinese army.

In mid-May of 1900, the Boxers burned down an Orthodox church and school in the village Dundin'yan. Then, "on the 23rd of May, the Boxers started entering Peking and began to unite with the regular army. The father of the heir to the Qing Dynasty called upon the people to exterminate the foreigners" [4, p. 35]. Facing the threat of reprisal, foreigners fled to the diplomatic quarters which withstood the Boxers' siege for several weeks. The Russian counsel convinced the head of the 18th Mission, Innocent Figurovsky, and the Russian clergy to move under the protection of the diplomatic mission. A territory of the Northern Compound was empty. Chinese Orthodox Christians from the nearby houses were trying to leave, but it was difficult to hide since neighbors and local citizens often pointed the Boxers in their direction.

Being left without spiritual direction, several Chinese parishioners, who seemed spiritually weak, struggling to keep their faith under the weight of pagan superstitions, at these moments demonstrated the miracle of martyric perseverance in the Christian faith. The majority of the Peking parishioners escaped to the house of the priest, Father Mitrophan Tzi (1855-1900). He was ordained in 1882 by St. Nicholas (Kasatkin) of Japan, in Tokyo, since at that time there was no Orthodox bishop in China, and became the first Orthodox priest of Chinese origin. "His acceptance of the priesthood was an act of heroism, for [even] at that time, it was more dangerous and difficult to be a Christian that at any time in Chinese history [to that point]. Anti-foreign and anti-Christian sentiments had grown strong in China in reaction to the colonial expansionism of Western European powers during the second half of the 19th century.

"[Even prior to the Boxer Rebellion,] outbreaks would occur, resulting in the deaths of foreigners and Chinese Christian converts."[20]

On June 10/23, 1900, the Boxers stormed the house of Fr. Mitrophan Tzi and killed the priest with swords. Together with him, they killed seventy more Chinese Orthodox Christians.

 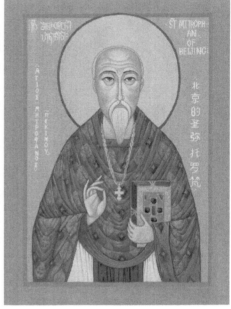

A photograph of Holy Hieromartyr Mitrophan Tzi (1855-1900), the first Orthodox priest of Chinese origin. He was ordained by St. Nicholas (Kasatkin) of Japan, in Tokyo, in 1882 (left). A canonical icon of Holy Hieromartyr Mitrophan Tzi (right).

After that, scores more Chinese Orthodox Christians were killed. The majority of them were killed by swords or by cutting off their heads. Some of them were required to worship idols in the pagan temple of Chenen'sy [33-15], others were tortured to death. For example, the Boxers cut off the shoulders and toes of an 8-year old boy, Ioann (John), Fr. Mitrophan's son, and cut the leg of the old teacher, Ia Kui Lin [33, p.16]. A servant at the male school of the Mission, Victor Fu, was killed and his heart was taken from his body and sacrificed to the flag by the Boxers [33, p.24]. The situation resembled the persecutions of Christians in the Roman Empire during the first centuries A.D. All the buildings of the Mission were destroyed and burned down.

---

[20] "Christ the Eternal Tao," by Hieromonk Damascene (2002), p. 434.

Icon of the Holy Martyr Ia Wen (left). A photograph of the catechist, the Holy Martyr Paul Wang, who was expected to be ordained a priest in 1900 (right).

Altogether, during the Boxer Rebellion, 222 Chinese Orthodox Christians were killed, a half of all the parishioners of that time. "The Orthodox had a greater loss in proportion to their numerical strength [in China] than did either the Roman Catholics or the Protestants."[21] Their relics were buried in the basement of the specially constructed Cathedral of All Saints in 1902.

This cathedral was destroyed in 1957, by the orders of the Soviet Counsel P.F. Yudin.[22] All the remaining possessions of the Mission and its library were also burned by the Soviet diplomats. According to the words of witnesses, it was very similar to the destruction of the Mission by the Boxers.

The relics of the Holy Martyrs were transferred to the cemetery church of St. Seraphim [30]. In 1986, the territory of the Orthodox cemetery in Beijing was turned into amusement park, Tsinnyakhu ("Youth Lake"). Now, a golf course has replaced the destroyed St. Seraphim Church.

---

[21] "Eastern Orthodox Mission Theology Today," by James J. Stamoolis (1986), p. 42.
[22] In 2007, a memorial cross was erected at the place of the All Saints Cathedral on the territory Russian Consulate in Beijing [26, p.50].

Altogether, 30,000 Chinese Roman Catholics, 2,000 Chinese Protestants, about 100 European missionaries and several diplomats were killed during the Boxer Rebellion of 1900 [6, p.261]. It led to military intervention in China by the forces of eight states including Russia, the United States, Germany, Great Britain, France, Japan, Austria-Hungary, and Italy. As a result, the Boxer Rebellion was put down. New agreements then reinforced the political dependence of China and eventually forced the fall of the Qing Dynasty in 1912.

As a result of the devastation wrought by the Boxer Rebellion, the very existence of the Russian Spiritual Mission in China became uncertain. However, the perseverance demonstrated by the head of 18th Mission, Father Innocent (Figurovsky), together with the principled position of the Metropolitan of St. Petersburg, Antony (Wadkovsky), influenced the final decision to preserve and restore the Mission. This decision stimulated new life in missionary work at the beginning of 20th century and led to a tremendous growth of Orthodoxy in China, comparable to the growth rate of other Christian confessions.

The President of the Brotherhood of All Chinese Saints, Mitrofan Nelson Chin, from Boston, stands at the place of the destroyed Cathedral of All Saints in Beijing (now on the territory of the Russian Consulate in China).

5. AN APOSTLE TO CHINA

Metropolitan Innocent (Figurovsky, 1863-1931), a doctor of theology,

was rector of the St. Petersburg Seminary and then head of 18th Spiritual Mission in China for thirty-four years (1897-1931). He has been justly called an "Apostle to China." At the beginning of his service in China, in 1897, there were only five churches and 458 Orthodox Chinese [34, p.86]. By his death in 1931, there were already 10,000 Orthodox Chinese and about 100 churches in China. Within the next three years, Orthodox churches would be built in Macao, Hong Kong, and Manila.

Metropolitan Innocent (Figurovsky, 1863-1931), Apostle to China.

During his work at the Mission, Father Innocent faced many challenges including the destruction and the rebuilding of the Mission in 1900, lawsuits with the Soviet government for the Mission's material possessions, and the yoke of responsibilities for taking care of Russian émigrés who had fled to China after the Russian Civil War.

When the Mission was destroyed by the members of the Boxer movement, Father Innocent went to live for a while in the nearby Buddhist (Lamaist) monastery of Yunghegun, where "one of the rooms was transformed into an Orthodox church" [8, p.146]. Because of his strong protection, the monastery was saved from destruction by German troops. As a sign of appreciation for his help, the Chinese authorities presented the Russian Mission with the gift of "Red Fansa," a nearby palace belonging to a local prince in disgrace. This building still exists on the territory of the Consulate of the Russian Federation in China.

"Red Fansa" – a house church used by the heads of the Russian Spiritual Mission in China, named after St. Innocent of Irkutsk. (Now it is on the territory of the Consulate of the Russian Federation in China.)

In 1902, Father Innocent became the first Orthodox bishop in China, with the title *Pereyaslavlsky* (of Pereyaslavl), the same title that Saint Innocent (Kulchitsky) of Irkutsk had 180 years before him. First of all, Bishop Innocent succeeded in achieving the economic and financial independence of the Mission. With the help of the restitution money paid by the Qing government for the Boxers' destruction of the Mission, a brickworks was opened, a flour store in the merchant lines of Peking market was purchased, and bindery and shoemaker shops were organized [6, p.266].

Five Mission representation centers (*metochia*) were opened in Russia, including centers in Moscow and St. Petersburg. In addition, the Mission bought several parcels of land in different regions of China with the purpose of organizing "missionary stations," where paid catechists were employed and chapels and schools for Chinese children were built.

Teachers and students of the missionary station school in Tunchzhou.

By 1912, there were nineteen schools for Chinese boys and two for Chinese girls [6, p.289]. New churches were built in many cities. Bishop Innocent himself, while traveling, used his sleeping car in the train as a missionary house [6, p.268]. One of the first tasks he undertook in 1902 was building the Cathedral of All Holy Martyrs to replace the destroyed Assumption Church in the Bayguan compound.

In 1903, five Orthodox nuns arrived in Peking from the Krasnoyarsk Monastery of the Holy Sign. In 1905, an Albazinian, Pelagia Markovna Zhui, became the first Orthodox nun of Chinese origin [6, p.267].

By 1916, the Russian Spiritual Mission had nineteen churches, thirty-two missionary stations, a seminary in Beijing, and eighteen male and three female schools with 700 students combined. At this time, there were 6,255

Orthodox Christians in China, with 706 baptisms held over the last year. In 1914, collections were started in order to build an Orthodox Cathedral in Beijing [34, p.106; 6, p. 299-300].

Russian Convent at Peking.

An Orthodox convent in Peking, on the territory of the Russian Mission, 1898.

This period of Orthodox revival in China at the beginning of the 20th century was also characterized by the beginning of the formation of the unique face of Chinese Orthodoxy. This portrait has not yet been fully defined in Russian historiography, and is awaiting its full investigation and understanding in the future by members of the autonomous Orthodox Church of China. Although, at this period, the Russian names still dominate among the church leaders, in 1914, in Beijing, there were forty-six missionaries of Chinese origin, compared to thirty-five missionaries of Russian origin [6, p.282].

In 1904, Sergei Chan, a son of the Holy Martyr Mitrofan Tzi, was ordained to the priesthood [6, p. 273].

Another priest, Mikhail Min, was ordained in 1908. He was head of the missionary station in the village of Dundin'yan [6, p.282], and later served in Tunchzhou, in the province of Czhili [8, p.294]. Another priest, Mikhail

Tan, took care of about 600 Orthodox Christians in the region of Yunpinfu [6, p.282]. By 1917, only Chinese missionaries were working in seventeen settlements in Hubaye [6, p. 294].

Protopresbyter Sergei Chan, a son of the Holy Hieromartyr Mitrofan Tzi (left) and Protopresbyter Mikhail Min, photo from 1951 (right).

6. "RUSSIAN ATLANTIS"

The character and activities of the Mission dramatically changed as a result of the Russian Civil War.[23] The Mission started focusing its activities on serving the needs of the Russian emigrants. This caused some discontent among the Chinese Orthodox. In 1919, due to a threat of bankruptcy, all the missionary stations were closed.

Canonically, in 1920 the Mission went under the Synod of the Russian Church Abroad. In 1922, a Beijing Diocese was established on the base of the Mission, with bishops in Shanghai (Bishop Simon Vinogradov) and Tientsin (Bishop Jonah Pokrovsky). Also, the Harbin Diocese was formed with vicarages in Hailarian and Manchuria. Later, the Tientsin cathedra was moved to Hankow, with Bishop Jonah (Pokrovsky) – called Hankowsky after his see. [34, p.127].

---

[23] The Russian Civil War (1917-22), was a period of violent instability following the Bolshevik Revolution. An estimated two million people were killed by war, disease, executions, and politically-motivated murder. Three million died from typhus alone after the war, and millions more died from starvation, disease, political murder, and pogroms. By 1922, there were seven million street children in Russia, orphans of the devastation. Around two million refugees fled Russia, moving through the Baltic countries, the Black Sea, and the Far East. These émigrés formed a large portion of the Russian Empire's educated and skilled population. Around 200,000 Russian émigrés settled in Harbin and about 25,000 in Shanghai, where they made up the largest European population. In 1920, the Chinese government ceased recognition of the Russian Imperial government, leaving the émigrés stateless. In 1924 the Chinese and Soviet governments signed an agreement forcing workers on the China Eastern Railway, the eastern end of the Trans-Siberian Railroad, to be Soviet or Chinese citizens. A faction of Russian émigrés working for the railroad accepted Soviet citizenship. This split the Russian émigrés in Harbin and led to greater Soviet influence in the Russian exile community. In 1945, the Soviet Army occupied Harbin and sent those deemed political enemies to labor camps.

Due to the large number of White Russian emigrants, Harbin was the epicenter of Russian culture in China for almost forty years, claiming the poetic name "Russian Atlantis." The Russian Harbin diaspora, composed of White Army soldiers, aristocracy, intelligentsia, artists, and ordinary people fleeing violence, tyranny, and economic devastation, included many famous names such as Chaliapin[24] and Vertinsky.[25]

Church wedding of Alexander Vertinsky and Lydia Tzirgvava in the main Cathedral of the Icon of the Mother of God "The Surety of Sinners," Shanghai, 1942.

Photograph from the cover of the Russian emigrant magazine "Rubezh," 1936. Dipping into the icy waters of the River Sungary in Harbin during the Feast of the Baptism of Our Lord (Theophany or Epiphany; in Russian, Krehschenie).

"Russian Atlantis" submerged into the past when the White Russians fled China in the 1950s, leaving behind a number of European buildings, and taking with them in their hearts the memories of a cultural oasis in a time of exile. Among those buildings left behind were 106 Orthodox churches.[26] Most of them were destroyed during Chinese Cultural Revolution.

---

[24] Feodor Chaliapin (1873-1938) – famous Russian bass, an opera singer.
[25] Alexander Vertinsky – famous Russian cabaret singer, poet, and composer.
[26] Data of 1949 [34, p.148].

Saint Nicholas Cathedral in Harbin. It was destroyed in 1966.

In general, "Russian Atlantis" did not play a significant role in missionary work. Though they were providentially positioned to preach the Orthodox faith, the Russian émigrés did not realize the potential for evangelism and did not care about preaching the Gospel to Chinese. Instead, a highly politicized emigration tried to engage the Church in various forms of political unions.

However, new Orthodox saints were revealed during this emigrant period. Among them are Blessed Jonah Hankowsky (Pokrovsky, 1888-1925) and Saint John (Maximovitch) the Wonderworker of Shanghai (1896-1966). Both of them were canonized by the Russian Orthodox Church Abroad.

After repose of Metropolitan Innocent (Figurovsky), Bishop Simon (Vinogradov) of Shanghai succeeded him as Archbishop of Beijing. He also became the head of the 19th Russian Spiritual Mission. In 1933, Bishop Victor (Svyatin) became the head of the Beijing Diocese. Later, he was made the Archbishop of Peking and the leader of 20th and last Russian Spiritual Mission, until its closing in 1956.[27]

---

[27] See Appendix I.

40

Saint Jonah (Pokrovsky),
Bishop of Hankow (+October 7/20, 1925)

Archimandrite Jonah (Pokrovsky) served as the main priest in the military divisions of Ataman Dutov and came to China with the remaining troops. In 1922, Jonah was consecrated the bishop of Tientsin in Manchuria, but later his cathedra was moved to Hankow. He started an orphanage for forty children. He established elementary, middle, and grade schools where up to 1,500 students could get free education. He organized a soup kitchen with free daily meals for 200 people and set up a free clinic where the poorest could get medical assistance and free medications. [34, p.121]. In addition, Bishop Jonah published theological brochures and gave lectures at the departments of theology and philosophy in Harbin. He was also invited by the Harbin City Council to teach catechism in the city schools. The students liked him so much that they demanded to be tested even though it was not required. They all demonstrated good knowledge of the subject [2].

According to ROCOR's 1996 Act of Canonization: "The entire three year ministry of Bishop Jonah was so filled with the fulfillment of Christ's main commandment of mercy that for someone else, even a good pastor, to do something similar would take decades. The scope and power of this ministry was remembered in Manchuria by Orthodox and pagans alike. To sum up Saint Jonah's ministry, Bishop Meletius, then Bishop of Zaibakalya,

41

wrote that he fulfilled the main commandment of Christ: he fed the hungry, gave drink to the thirsty, took in the wayfarers, clothed the poor and visited the sick ... The fulfillment of this commandment, prepared for by lifelong asceticism, was the content of the entire life of Bishop Jonah."[28]

Icon of the Blessed Jonah Hankowsky (Pokrovsky)

Saint John (Maximovitch) the Wonderworker, Bishop of Shanghai (+June 19/July 2, 1966)

Saint John (Maximovitch) the Wonderworker and Bishop of Shanghai was known as a man of strict asceticism since the early days of his life as a monk in Serbia. In 1934, he was consecrated a bishop by Metropolitan Antony (Khrapovitsky) and sent to Shanghai. In Shanghai, he built the main cathedral of the Icon of the Mother of God "The Surety of Sinners" and the Saint Nicolas Church in memory of the Passion-Bearer Tsar Nicolas II. St. John also established an orphanage dedicated to St. Tikhon of Zadonsk, which cared for three and a half thousand orphaned children, both Chinese and Russian. Many of them were brought there by Saint John personally through his many excursions through the slums of Shanghai. During his Shanghai years, he became known as "the Wonderworker" on account of his many miracles in healing the sick and helping the poor.

---

[28] Fr. Denis Pozdnyaev, "The Russian Ecclesiastical Mission, 1920-1930." (http://www.academia.edu/5692240/The_Russian_Ecclesiastical_Mission_1920-1930). All texts quoted from this source have been edited.

"People loved Bishop John for his manifold charitable activities. All the community initiatives of Russian Shanghai – the building of a hospital, shelters, schools, homes for the elderly, communal dining rooms, and a commercial school – all this was accomplished with his blessing and his personal participation."[29]

Due to the Communist Revolution, Bishop John (Maximovitch), left China in 1949 for the Philippines with many of his parishioners. From there, after several years in Europe, he came to the United States, where he was made head of the San Francisco Archdiocese.

A photograph (above) and a canonical icon (below) of Saint John (Maximovitch) the Wonderworker of Shanghai, 1896-1966.

St. John himself was missionary-minded. He was known to celebrate the Divine Liturgy in Chinese. Several native Chinese priests also served in his diocese, including Fr. Elias Wen, who fled China after the Communist takeover in 1949, and later emigrated to the United States.

---

[29] Ibid.

Innocent (Figurovsky), Metropolitan of
Beijing (+June 15/28, 1931)

Like a pelican pricking its own breast to feed her young, the Mission, itself already in difficult material circumstances, sacrificed itself to care for the refugees fleeing Russia.

Fr. Denis Pozdnayev notes:[30]

"Deprived of financial help from Russia, from the income of the representation churches in Moscow and Petrograd, and burdened with debt, the Mission was in a state of almost total collapse. The pitiable condition of the Mission was worsened by the plots of Archbishop Innocent's enemies. Many disliked his intolerance of democracy ... On the anniversary of the Revolution in Russia, Archbishop Innocent wrote: 'They try to suggest to us that the Church should not interfere in politics. This is the baldest lie. [They say that] the Church should not get involved in political squabbles, should be above all political parties, and yet they overturn thrones and shake the foundations of the state. In their hands, governments are marionettes...And what kind of loyalty can one speak of when, for obedience to today's authorities, one can be shot by the new authority tomorrow? ... If we are Christians, then in reply to the violence of the Bolsheviks toward the Church, we must cut off any contact with them ... God's anger towards us will not be turned away from us until we repent.'

At that time, the religious life of Harbin, a city settled by artisans and workers of the Chinese Eastern Railway, was in decline. Sects flourished among the early Russian emigrants and many were swayed to Theosophy, which, as Archbishop Innocent himself wrote, is a denial of belief in the Lord Jesus Christ as God.

The following illustrates the anemic state of Orthodoxy in Manchuria at that time. In 1922, only six out of 250 Orthodox families in the Zaton area of Harbin received a priest making visits in a procession at Christmas. This coldness of the Russian Orthodox emigrants toward Church life would get to such a point that, in 1928, the Roman pope would send a Uniate bishop to proselytize among them. This dire spiritual situation was only changed in Harbin by the arrival of many Russian Orthodox clergy and monks. In 1922, the Diocese of Harbin was organized as an entity separate from the Mission.

---

[30] Ibid.

Beside the external pressure from sectarians and heterodox, there were also divisions among the Orthodox in China. Archbishop Innocent's enemies—and he had several within the Church—used weakened mission outreach to the local population as an excuse for fomenting dissatisfaction among the Chinese Orthodox clergy and laity, to the point of reforming the governance of the Church.

During this time of upheaval, there was little to no unity of mind among the clergy and the parishioners in China—both Chinese and Russian. Instead, there were factions among the clergy and disputes between parishioners and bishops over property. Archbishop Innocent had the good will for bringing about a better unity and cooperation, but competing parties and antagonistic agendas thwarted his efforts."[31]

Archbishop Innocent was raised to the rank of metropolitan in 1928. By then, he was already nearing the end of his earthly life. In his zeal for truth, he fought hard against the evils of heresy, schism, and vice.

"He summoned all to unite under the shelter of the Church and thundered against the unbelief, lawlessness and wantonness of part of the Russian emigration. Metropolitan Innocent was a strong defender of the unity of the Church and the immutability of its canons."[32]

Metropolitan Innocent was also given to know beforehand the day of his death.

"The night before his death, the metropolitan had a dream in which he saw many clergy, clothed in vestments and carrying icons, coming into his room toward him. The Metropolitan asked: 'Why have you come to me with icons?' Someone answered: 'To bury you.'

"Bishop Simon, the future head of the Mission, also had a dream before he came to visit the dying metropolitan. He saw him sitting in the area in front of the metropolitan's quarters. Suddenly a bird flew up, carrying a blossoming branch, then changed into the image of an angel with blossoming branches in his arms. Bishop Simon said to someone: 'It is an angel.' And someone replied: 'Yes, it is one of the twelve.' The metropolitan saw these dreams as a portent of his death. He reposed on June 28, 1931.

"On the anniversary of the death of Metropolitan Innocent, in his

---

[31] Ibid.
[32] Ibid.

45

sermon Archbishop Simon said: 'The late Metropolitan Innocent especially revered the day of his consecration as a bishop as the day of the foundation of Christ's Church in China, but not June 3, but on the Day of the Holy Spirit, the second day of the feast of Pentecost, which fell on that date that year... According to the Liturgy of the Orthodox Church, when a new church is being built, the relics of the martyrs are laid under the altar by the hands of the bishop. So, too, the remains of those Chinese who had suffered as martyrs for the Orthodox faith were collected by the hands of the late Metropolitan Innocent and buried on the land of the Mission in Peking."[33]

Simon (Vinogradov), Archbishop of Beijing (+January 29/February 11, 1933)

Arcbishop Simon came to China as a young hieromonk in 1902.

"Having arrived in Peking, he zealously undertook missionary service and the restoration of the property of the Mission, which had been destroyed during the Boxer Rebellion. For a while, he served at the representation church of the Mission in Harbin. On the feast of the Dormition of the Most Holy Theotokos in 1907, he was raised to the dignity of archimandrite, and on September 17, 1922, his ordination to Bishop of Shanghai, first vicar of the Beijing diocese, took place. With the appearance of Russian emigrants in China, Bishop Simon displayed particular care for his suffering countrymen.

"Archbishop Simon showed himself to be an image of humility and obedience. A zealous man of prayer, he was an ascetic his whole life, trying to be inconspicuous. His outstanding trait, besides asceticism and complete humility, was his strictness to himself in regard to fulfillment of his duties. To those close to him he always maintained a loving and good-hearted attitude. He had a gift for words. Many remember him as an elder, one who had attained spiritual peace and was adorned with spiritual insight."[34]

After the death of Metropolitan Innocent (Figurovsky) in 1931, the Bishop of Shanghai, Simon (Vinogradov), became the Archbishop of Beijing, and continued to be in the position for the next two years. During this time, a schism in the Chinese Orthodox Church occurred since Archpriest Sergei Chan, who considered himself the successor of Metropolitan Innocent, made a decision to join Russian Orthodox Church

---

[33] Ibid.

[34] Ibid.

under the Patriarch of Moscow. Father Sergei was followed by a group of Chinese Orthodox who built the Saint Innocent Church in Tientsin, where all the priests and clergy were Chinese. It was the first attempt of the Orthodox Chinese to arrange church autonomy.

"Fr. Sergei believed that the fundamental task of the Mission, the preaching Orthodoxy among the Chinese, had been unfairly replaced, in his view, with care for the Russian emigrants."

Despite the machinations of those who love controversies, "it was a special concern of Archbishop Simon that a permanent church be established in Shanghai. In 1932, a Japanese shell fell on the bell tower of the old Theophany Cathedral and started a fire, which then destroyed the first Orthodox church in Shanghai. Only the sacred vessels and an insignificant part of the church plate escaped destruction.

"The Japanese authorities, although they acknowledged their fault and promised to rebuild the church, forgot their promise after they occupied Shanghai.

"The completion of the construction of the new cathedral in honor of the Icon of the Most Holy Theotokos 'Surety of Sinners,' which took place under the direction of St. John the Wonderworker, was Archbishop Simon's last testament. He said: 'The Lord permitted the destruction of our church. Awaiting our repentance, the Lord allowed us to build a prayer house, but if we think that we can get by without a church, the anger of God will not delay and one day we will be deprived of our prayer houses, and we will be left to wander in the darkness which we have loved more than the light…The Russian community, if it approaches the construction of a church with faith and unanimity, will be blessed before God. The Athos icon of the Mother of God was sent to China in 1903. In 1926, it was given to me as a blessing on my departure from Shanghai. This icon is called
'Surety of Sinners' as is written on the icon itself. The Most Holy Virgin Mary intercedes for sinners before God for their correction and promises her help to all those who seek it.'

"Archbishop Simon was not fated to complete the construction of the cathedral. In the middle of February 1933, he caught a cold while blessing the site of the Shanghai cathedral. The illness progressed, and on February 24, he died peacefully. His body was transferred to Beijing and buried in the crypt of the right gallery of the Church of All Holy Martyrs, next to the place of burial of Metropolitan Innocent. When the coffin with his remains was transferred in 1940, it was observed that his holy relics were incorrupt.

He was one of the ascetics of piety and 'a standard of faith and an image of meekness."' [35]

Victor (Svyatin),
Archbishop of Beijing (+September 5/18, 1966)[36]

Archbishop Victor arrived in China in 1919 with the White Russian Army of General Bakich. From his youth, he had been inclined toward monasticism. In 1921, he finally became a monk at the Dormition Monastery in Peking. Seeing in him a potential for leadership, Metropolitan Innocent sent Fr. Victor to Vladivostok to further his studies, however political upheavals there forced him to return to China in 1922. After recovering from typhoid fever, he took monastic vows, was ordained as a hieromonk, and sent to be a parish priest in Tientsin (Tianjin), where he served for ten years.

Archbishop Victor (Svyatin), the head of the last Russian Spiritual Mission in China.

There, he became well known through his care of Russian emigrants and compatriots, establishing a gymnasium, a nursing home, a hospital and a soup kitchen. He cared for dozens of homeless people who found a place in his apartments commonly referred as "Victor's hotel" [22, p.41].

In 1933, Bishop Victor (Svyatin) became the head of the Beijing Diocese. Later, he was made the Archbishop of Beijing and the leader of 20th and last Russian Spiritual Mission, until its closing in 1956.

---

[35] Ibid.
[36] Some information in this section comes from this site:
http://www.orthodox.cn/localchurch/beijing/lastchiefvictor_en.txt.

In 1944, Archbishop Victor asked Moscow Patriarch Sergei (Stargorodsky) about the Beijing Diocese joining the Moscow Patriarchate, which later happened in 1945. Bishop John (Maximovitch) in Shanghai remained under the Russian Church Abroad. At this point, the ways of two outstanding church hierarchs diverged.

The 1949 Communist takeover in China brought an end to the free operation of foreign missionaries. Archbishop Victor was faced with the serious challenge of how to ensure that Church life could continue without Russian support. There seemed no other way to do this than try to establish a Chinese Orthodox Church, which would be recognized by the state.

"Archbishop Victor suggested dividing the Mission's activity into five main aspects: missionary (the preaching of Orthodoxy among the Chinese population), monastic, cultural, economic and charitable. There were plans to establish a vital link with theological schools in Russia, organize theological training in Beijing for Chinese priests, reopen missionary camps that had been closed under Metropolitan Innocent at the beginning of Russian emigration to China, found theological academies in Beijing, Tianjin, and Shanghai, as well as create a mission to translate theological literature into Chinese.

"Cultural and educational activity was to consist of opening Russian primary schools, publishing Russian-Chinese periodicals, organizing various lectures and courses, and opening new libraries at the missionary camps and in the parishes."[37]

This was a very ambitious program, and while Archbishop Victor supported it, support from Church authorities in Russia was lackluster. There were no funds available.

In the end, the property of the Mission was divided between the Communist Chinese government and the Soviet embassy. The Mission was closed and the native Chinese Orthodox were, essentially, left to fend for themselves. The Cultural Revolution that was to come would destroy this nascent dream for a Chinese Orthodox Church.

In 1956, Archbishop Victor (Svyatin) returned to Russia and was appointed Archbishop of Krasnodar and Kuban. In 1961, he was raised to the rank of metropolitan. After a brief illness and heart attack, he reposed in 1966.

---

[37] http://www.orthodox.cn/localchurch/pozdnyaev/4_en.htm

Archbishop Victor (Svyatin) and a group of Chinese Orthodox by the "Red Fanza" at the Mission (currently, a territory of the Russian Consulate in China), Beijing, 1955.

7. NOTABLE MONASTICS IN CHINA

Along with higher clergy, soldiers, aristocrats, intellectuals and ordinary people, there were also many monks and nuns who fled persecution by the Communists in Russia. Many of these were witnesses to martyrdom. Following the word of the Lord, "When they persecute you in this city, flee ye into another" (Matthew 10:23), these monastics came to China and established new monasteries as homes for themselves and the precious relics they carried with them, and also as centers of spiritual support for orphans, the Russian exile community, and the local Chinese. Among these monastics were Abbess Rufina of Harbin and Shanghai, Schemamonk[38] Michael of Harbin, Schemahieromonk[39] Ignatius of Harbin, and others whose names are more widely remembered than the details of their lives.

Abbess Rufina of Harbin and Shanghai
(+August 15/28, 1937)[40]

Abbess Rufina's journey into exile from Russia began in June of 1919, when troops of the White Army occupied the town of Cherdyn, where her convent of St. John the Theologian was located. When the army retreated, Abbess Rufina and her sisters abandoned their convent and fled the advancing Red Army, traveling in a railroad freight car. In August, the train found the Mary and Martha Sisterhood as a traveling convent. She accepted

---

[38] Schemamonk: A monk who has taken the great schema. In the Russian tradition, the great schema is given after a monk or nun has spent many years in the monastic life, before he or she enters into greater seclusion, or when he or she is at the point of death.

[39] Schemahieromonk: A priest-monk who has taken the great schema.

[40] Most of the material on Abbess Rufina comes from an account by Abbess Ariadna, her successor, from this site: http://stvladimirs.ca/wordpress/the-life-of-abbess-rufina-royal-path-of-a-great-struggler/.

51

150 children into a traveling orphanage and nursery. Forced to retreat again, Abbess Rufina, with her sisters, obtained a freight car in the army column and moved east to Chita. An epidemic of typhus broke out among the sisters and the sick were left to recover at a convent in Chita.

In February1920, Abbess Rufina arrived in Vladivostok. There, she was given four acres of land behind the city cemetery to start a new convent. For three years, the sisters tended to the graves in the cemetery, supported themselves through their handiwork, and prayed the services of the Church. Then, it became necessary to abandon even this refuge. Abbess Rufina and her sisters arrived in Harbin, Manchuria at the beginning of June 1923, where she established the Convent of the Vladimir Icon of the Mother of God, known originally as the Tikhvin Convent.

In its first years, the convent faced many difficulties. The nuns lacked everything and had to work day and night without rest since their only source of income was their own handiwork, prosphora (bread for the Eucharist) baking, and doing laundry. Yet God blessed these years of toil and hardship.

An unknown pious elderly lady brought to the convent an old and damaged icon of the Vladimir Mother of God on its feast day, August 26, 1924. The woman told the novice who received the icon that she couldn't throw it away, in spite of its condition. The icon was quite old and so darkened by time and soot so that its features could not be seen easily.

Abbess Rufina accepted the icon and set it in a prominent place in the convent church, which at the time had very few icons. Some people complained about the icon's lackluster condition, so it was moved behind the iconostasis and placed in a corner. There, the icon was criticized by the clergy.

But exactly one year later, on August 26, 1925, the Most Holy Theotokos showed everyone what she thought of her icon. At two o'clock in the afternoon on the feast of the "Vladimirskaya" Icon of the Mother of God, when several people were to be released from prison, Abbess Rufina decided to bless them with the icon. The icon was brought to her from the altar and, when it was placed in her hands, it quickly began to lighten, the way that fog scatters in the sunlight. All the dust and grime that had settled on it with the passing of time simply disappeared. The darkened colors brightened and the image became visible again. After only a few minutes, the icon looked as though it had just been painted. Holding the holy icon, Abbess Rufina exclaimed, "Look, look, a miracle is taking place. The icon is being restored!"[41]

A moleben (prayer service) was served by one of the hieromonks of the convent, who only a few days earlier had recommended that the icon be burned and the ashes thrown into the river. Seeing the miracle, he begged forgiveness from the Mother of God with tears.

The miracle strengthened the sisters' faith, assuring them that the Mother of God was truly their guardian and directress. Metropolitan Meletius blessed changing the convent's name to that of the Vladimir Icon of the Mother of God.

The Miraculous Renewal of the Vladimir Icon of the Most Holy Theotokos in the hands of the righteous Abbess Rufina of Harbin is annually commemorated in the Orthodox Church on August 26.

Life at the convent was very strict. The nuns followed an austere rule centered on prayer, gathering in the church twelve times a day, with no service lasting less than half an hour. But, just as they had before assisted orphans and other suffering refugees in Russia, the sisterhood also assisted in caring for a new wave of Russian refugees.

In 1929, Soviet forces in the Far East crossed the border into China and, in Trekhreche, fell upon Russian refugees with savage cruelty. Metropolitan Anthony Khrapovitsky wrote: "Whole villages of Russians were destroyed, the male population was decimated, women and children were raped and killed. No mercy was shown to age, sex, the weak, the ill. The entire Russian population, unarmed, was killed, shot with terrifying cruelty and senseless torture." Refugees from the attacks in Trekhreche fled to Harbin, and many of them were cared for by Abbess Rufina and her nuns, who cared for over 600 orphaned girls since leaving their original home in Cherdyn.

Despite having a recurring illness, Abbess Rufina loved to spend whole nights in prayer, preparing her soul for its departure from the body. God granted her the gift of prophecy and clairvoyance.

---

[41] The miracle of self-renewing icons has been witnessed countless times all over the globe. No products are used. No curators are employed. The icons simply lighten, becoming like they were on the day they were painted. Sometimes they also darken by themselves. This phenomenon occurred with at least five different icons in China during the 20th

century. It calls to mind St. Paul's words, "Be not conformed to this world: but be ye transformed by the renewing of your mind, that ye may prove what is that good, and acceptable, and perfect will of God" (Romans 12:2).nce, a young man in Harbin came under the influence of the intellectuals of his time, seeing "progress" in Communism, and lost his faith in God. Unsure of the existence of God, he decided no longer to wear a Cross around his neck. Shortly thereafter, his father died and the young man was shaken again.

He had heard of Abbess Rufina, and so decided to go to the convent for Divine Liturgy. The kindness and accessibility of Abbess Rufina won his heart. After showing him to her office and exchanging the usual introductory formalities, she looked deep into his eyes and said, "There is something I must do for you, but I have forgotten what." She began to think, and the young man was silent and said nothing about his Cross because he thought Abbess Rufina wasn't feeling well. Suddenly she exclaimed, "Oh yes!" and jumped up and called a nun and said something quietly to her. Through the door, the young man could hear Mother Rufina ask the nun to bring something to her. Having returned to her office, Abbess Rufina began to murmur a prayer. When the sister returned with something in her hand, the abbess approached the young man, her eyes shining joyfully, and said, "Here, I prepared for you a little Cross. The only trouble is I don't have a chain, but that's all right. I'll take the one from my own Cross."

About this incident the young man said, "I cannot express what my soul experienced. Only a man who gains back his faith could understand it."

Several times, as early as 1927, Abbess Rufina warned her sisters that the time would come when they would have to leave Harbin as well, and should prepare to move the convent to America – that God was leading them there. The eight thousand mile move was not possible at that time, so instead the sisterhood moved to Shanghai, and founded a new convent, as well as an orphanage for girls.

At the end of her life, Abbess Rufina would often receive visits and Holy Communion from St. John (Maximovitch). On his last visit, Bishop John stood there for a long time and awaited her death. On that occasion, the abbess said peacefully, "Everything is finished, I will go to a new apartment." She read Psalms and stichera for the feast of the Dormition of the Mother of God, and then said, "The bells are ringing. They sing beautifully. There are lots of people. Hurry up, let me go."

Just before her death, Abbess Rufina said, "God's great mercy was given to mankind, limitless mercy and love does the Mother of God show to us sinners, yet we are deaf and blind to the Divine Voice of Love.... We here, outside of Russia, more and more, are summoning upon ourselves the righteous wrath of the Judge. There is no peace or love in our hearts. If all of us, exiles from our native land, would fall down with a mighty cry before the miracle-working icon of the Heavenly Queen, and with one voice and heart exclaim to her thus: 'O Mother of God, save the Russian land and save us!' Then wouldn't she hear us? Oh yes, my beloved ones! She will hear us! She will obtain for us, from her beloved Son, the possibility of changing His wrath to mercy. If we only repent and give a promise to direct our lives according to the commandments of God." These were the words of righteous Abbess Rufina before her blessed repose in the early morning of August 15/28, 1937.

Abbess Ariadna, her successor, relates that often the departed Abbess Rufina has appeared in visions and dreams, calling people to prayer and to help those with needs. She has also appeared with words of consolation and instruction.

Abbess Ariadna relates one such case where Abbess Rufina appeared three times to a woman in St. Louis, Missouri, who was seriously ill. Abbess Rufina told her to pray in order to strengthen the state of her soul and body.

Schemamonk Michael of Harbin
(+December 21/January 1, 1939)

He was a starets[42] at the men's Monastery of the Kazan Icon of the Mother of God.

Schemahieromonk Ignatius (Melekhin) of Harbin
(+Autust 3/16, 1958)

He was the confessor at the men's Monastery of the Kazan Icon of the Mother of God in Harbin, starting in 1922. He was blind, but God gave him the gift of clairvoyance. He reposed on August 3/16, 1958.

---

[42] Starets: An elder, that is, an experienced and trustworthy spiritual guide, usually a monastic, and usually a priest and confessor, though not always.

In 1949, the People's Republic of China was established, and Russian emigrants started to leave China. Some of them believed in Soviet propaganda and decided to return to Russia. Others simply felt a longing for their homeland, which had been under attack in World War II. Upon coming home, most of them were sent into exile to the Kazakhstan deserts. There were also those who were forcibly deported to the Soviet Union. Others, witnessing a similarity between the Soviet and the new Chinese Communist regime, left for Australia, New Zealand, Europe, and America.

Two examples of returnees were Metroplitan Nestor (Anisimov) of Kamchatka, who returned voluntarily to be with the suffering homeland, and Archbishop Juvenaly (Kilin) of Tsitsikar, who was forcibly repatriated.

Nestor (Anisimov),
Metropolitan of Kirovgrad and Nikolaevsk,
Englightener of Kamchatka (+October 22/November 4, 1962)[43]

By the time he arrived in China in the early 1920s with the other White Russian refugees, Archbishop Nestor was already a veteran missionary, possessing considerable experience in making difficult journeys to dangerous places. As a young hieromonk in 1907-08, he preached the Word of God to the heathens of Kamchatka, such as the Kamchadals. He was diligent to the point of risking his own life to take care of his flock. He loved them dearly and greatly respected their customs and traditions and learned their languages. Yet, he realized that he could not, by himself, administer to their needs.

"He understood that with his small strength he could not solve all the problems in the all-but-abandoned region of Kamchatka. It was necessary to draw the attention of the powerful of the world, of the Church hierarchy, of the honest people who wanted to help their fellow men, those suffering from poverty, illness, drunkenness and the rapacity of local officials. Thus came about his idea to form the charitable Kamchatkan Brotherhood.

"From 1910-1917, at the expense of the Kamchatkan Brotherhood, dozens of churches, chapels, schools, shelters, hospitals, leprosy colonies, and ambulance stations were built. Having learned the Tungus (Evenki) and Koryak languages, Hieromonk Nestor translated the Divine Liturgy, parts of the Gospels, and selected prayers. For that work, Fr. Nestor was elevated to the rank of hegumen in 1913."

---

[43] Information from: Fr. Denis Pozdnayev, "The Russian Ecclesiastical Mission, 1920-1930." (http://www.academia.edu/5692240/The_Russian_Ecclesiastical_Mission_1920-1930).

The First World War would call Fr. Nestor from his mission field to the other side of the world. On the Russian front lines, he "organized and headed the hospital unit 'First Aid Under Fire,' and personally evacuated the wounded from the battlefield, taking care of their wounds, comforting them, and arranging their transport to field hospitals. For his altruistic and heroic work, Hegumen Nestor was awarded the prestigious religious and military honor, the right to wear a chest cross on a St. George's ribbon, as well as number of military medals.

"At the end of 1915, Fr. Nestor was demobilized from the front, elevated to the rank of archimandrite, and finally continued his pastoral mission in Kamchatka. On October 16, he was consecrated a bishop and was appointed the first ruling hierarch of the newly formed Kamchatka Diocese."

Arriving in Harbin, Archbishop Nestor founded the Joy of All Who Sorrow Kamchatka Representation Church in 1921, and the House of Mercy and Diligence on the church grounds in 1925. The House of Mercy operated a shelter for female orphans and aged widows and also ran an icon painting workshop. There was a chapel in the entrance erected in memory of the late Russian Emperor Nicholas II and King Alexander I of Yugoslavia.

"The House of Mercy helped preserve the lives of thousands of children and adults alike, caught in the chaos of the civil war. Being under the auspices of the Synod Abroad, Vladika Nestor painfully went through the turmoil of the 1920s and '30s, subsequently supporting the idea of the unity of the suffering Mother Church. During that period, the Archbishop visited many countries of Europe and Asia, meeting the hierarchs of the Russian Orthodox Church Abroad, the heads of many local Orthodox Churches, and the heads of some heterodox churches. On a number of occasions, he made pilgrimages to the Holy Land. In 1938-1939, he undertook missionary work in India and Ceylon (Sri Lanka).

"In 1948, after returning to Russia, Vladika Nestor was arrested and exiled to the prison camps. He was sentenced because of his participation in the transfer of the relics of Holy Martyr Elizabeth Romanov, the sister of the martyred Tsarina Alexandra,[44] the organizing of the Local Council in Vladivostok in 1922,

---

[44] The relics of the New Martyr St. Elizabeth and those who were martyred with her were brought from Alapayevsk in Siberia to China with the White Army. When the Soviets and the Communist Chinese worked to end the influence of the White Russians and the Orthodox Mission in China, the relics of the new martyrs were hidden by Archbishop Victor (Svyatin) and smuggled out of the country with the assistance of Archbishop Nestor. The holy relics of Sts. Elizabeth and Barbara now rest in Jerusalem.

the publishing of the book 'Shooting of the Moscow Kremlin,' the building of a chapel dedicated to the Crowned Martyrs [Tsar Nicholas II and his family, who had been executed by the Soviets in 1918]—activities which the Soviets deemed political crimes."

He was appointed Metropolitan of Novosibirsk and Barnaul in 1956, after his release. Then, in 1958, he was appointed Metropolitan of Kirovograd and Nikolaevsk. He reposed on October 22/November 4, 1962, and was buried in the courtyard of the church of the Patriarchal representation of Holy Trinity-Sergius Lavra in Peredelkino.

Juvenaly (Kilin), in schema, John, Archbishop of Izhevsk (+December 15/28, 1958)[45]

The Bolshevik Revolution of 1917 found Vladika Juvenaly as an archimandrite serving in the Diocese of Perm.

"Archbishop Andronik of Perm, Archimandrite Varlaam, and many other clergy were martyred, including over 400 monastics from Belogorsk. In 1918, Fr. Juvenaly and a few monastics from Belogorsk hid from the Bolsheviks - following the words of Christ: 'But when they persecute you in this city, flee ye into another' (Matt: 10:23).

"In 1919, Fr. Juvenaly moved to the Far East, first to Chita in Siberia, and then to Harbin in Manchuria in 1920. After arriving in Harbin, he was appointed rector in the Church of the Dormition and supervisor of a new Russian cemetery. In 1922, he established a men's monastery on Krestovsky Island with the blessing of Archbishop Methodius of Harbin. He was soon transferred to Serbia to be the superior of an Orthodox monastery.

"In 1924, he returned to Harbin and was blessed to start a new monastery dedicated to the Kazan Mother of God. There, he built a cathedral with three altars in honor of the Kazan Icon of the Mother of God. The monastery included monastic cells, a print shop, and a hospital.

"The monastery printshop issued a spiritual-moral periodical, *Khleb Nebesniy*, "Bread of Heaven." For ten years, Vladika Juvenaly served as the editor. Besides the printshop, the monastery had other workshops for icon painting, furniture making, bookbinding, shoemaking, and tailoring.

---

[45] From Fr. Denis Pozdnayev, "The Russian Ecclesiastical Mission, 1920-1930," edited.

"The monastery hospital that Vladika Juvenaly established provided medical treatment free of charge. It was established in memory of Dr. V.A. Kazem-Bek, who never charged a fee. Each year, on the eve of August 4, the day Dr. Kazem-Bek's repose, the monastery cathedral held a memorial service with a large number of clergy and laypeople attending. This was followed on the day itself with a liturgy and pannikhida over the doctor's grave. He had died at an early age from diphtheria contracted from a child patient.

"In 1934, the Holy Synod elected Fr. Juvenaly to be Bishop of Xinjiang, where Russian refugees kept the Tabinskaya Icon of the Mother of God and built several churches. The Orthodox residents of Ürümqi had suffered much from the Bolsheviks, and so the council appointed Fr. Juvenaly as an archpastor for them to support them and to solidify their diocesan and church life.

"Having received this decision by the Council, Archimandrite Juvenaly, preparing for his consecration, performed Divine Liturgy every day in the monastery Cathedral.

"He was consecrated on February 10, 1935, in St. Nicholas Cathedral in Harbin by the celebrants Archbishops Meletius of Harbin and Manchuria and Nestor of Kamchatka and Petropavlovsk, Bishops Dimitri of Hailar and St. John (Maximovich) of Shanghai, who was the first vicar of the Beijing Mission.

"After his consecration, Bishop Juvenaly found it was unfortunately impossible to travel to his remote new see, so he continued as superior of the Kazan Icon of the Mother of God Monastery until in 1936, when he administered the Beijing diocese for Bishop Victor while he was in Belgrade. From 1937-1938, Bishop Juvenaly acted for Bishop John of Shanghai while the latter was visiting the Synod of Bishops in Sremski Karlovci, Yugoslavia. After St. John's return, Bishop Juvenaly was attached to St. Nicholas Memorial Church in Shanghai and participated in the work of the Mission.

"In 1940, the Synod of Bishops of the Russian Church Abroad transferred Bishop Juvenaly to Tsitsikar in Manchuria. There, he continued to lead a strict ascetic life, drawing many worshipers to church through his astute teachings and love for the proper order of the services.

"'Vladyka Juvenaly,' recounts L.V. Shabardina, 'loved our church services. During vigil at the monastery, he would emerge in the middle of the church during the 9th ode of the canon and he would say, "Everyone sing!" The whole church then sang, and this seemed to refresh the worshipers. When Vladyka served, he immersed himself entirely in the service and fervently prayed, drawing others into a prayerful mood with his pious service. For this reason, we who prayed didn't tire.'

"The end of World War II and the occupation of Manchuria by Soviet forces again changed Bishop Juvenaly's life. In 1947, he was forced to go to the USSR, where he was appointed Bishop of Chelyabinsk. Arriving in Moscow, he heard of the death of Archbishop Dimitry (Voznesensky), the father of the future Metropolitan Philaret, First Hierarch of the Russian Orthodox Church Outside of Russia, and immediately left for Leningrad to attend his funeral and burial. In 1948, Vladyka Juvenaly was elevated to the rank of archbishop and appointed to Irkutsk, and a year later, to the Omsk cathedra, where he was the first bishop of that diocese after its reestablishment. As Archbishop of Omsk, Vladyka performed the transfer of the holy relics of St. John, Metropolitan of Tobolsk (and an ancestor of St. John the Wonderworker of Shanghai), to a new crypt. The clergy of the Omsk Diocese still remember Vladyka as a Spirit-bearing elder. In 1952, Vladyka was transferred to the Izhevsk and Udmurtsk cathedra.

"There, Vladyka Juvenaly began to feel his health declining. Foreseeing his death, he asked Archimandrite Peter (Semyonovykh) from Holy Trinity-St. Sergius Lavra to tonsure him into the great schema. He was tonsured and named John, after the apostle, evangelist, and theologian.

"Archbishop Juvenaly fell ill late in 1958. On December 25, he was given the Sacrament of Unction. On December 27, he donned his schema robes. On December 28, 1958, he asked his friends in attendance to sing the prokeimenon: 'Chant unto our God, chant ye; chant unto our King, chant ye,' three times. He reposed saying, 'Here is our new land, here is our new world.'

"The former cell-attendant of Vladyka Juvenaly, the Protopriest Nikolai Soloviev, said that, before his death, Vladyka asked to be allowed to retire due to failing strength. Patriarch Alexei I asked him to remain at his post and even offered him the title of metropolitan, but Archbishop Juvenaly declined the honor, saying that he did not serve to gain rank and that monasticism was more important for him.

"In his lifetime, Archbishop Juvenaly was responsible for converting at least one prominent Communist atheist. The commissar, Arkadii Arkadievich, despite his duties, was a believer, and had icons hung in his house, with oil lamps burning in front of them. He loved and supported Vladyka very much. Archbishop Juvenaly was the one who had converted him to the faith.

"'In his life, Vladyka was humble,' remembers Fr. Nikolai. 'He loved to joke, but he was also strict. He tried to hide his sagacity. A light often burned in his cell late at night, and during holidays he gave his cell attendants 25-50 rubles to distribute among the poor.' (In those times, that was a significant amount)."

Archbishop Juvenaly, besides being exceedingly generous, also had the gift of foresight. "In his youth, Fr. Nikolai wished to go to seminary. Together with other lads, he traveled to Moscow. Vladyka gave everyone money for a one-way ticket, but gave Nikolai enough to get there and back. Before this, he implored him to stay behind and bury him first, but Nikolai was stubborn. Finally, all the other young men joined the seminary, but Nikolai failed his exams and returned to Izhevsk. While Nikolai was still on his way to Vladyka's house, Vladyka three times instructed the house manager, Anastasia Aleksandrovna, to go meet Nikolai, but she said that he would only return during winter recess. The third time, she finally went, and turning the corner, she saw him coming. Thus, he was able to participate in the archbishop's funeral.

"The late archpastor is widely respected among the old Harbinites of the Russian Church Abroad and the clergy and faithful in Russia. Many stream to his crypt in the Izhevsk Cathedral and appeal to him for prayerful intercession, sensing his grace-filled help. A few years ago, Archbishop Nikolai of Izhevsk and Udmurtsk (ROC/MP) performed the translation of Archbishop Juvenaly's holy relics, during which it was discovered that his body was uncorrupt. The Diocese of Izhevsk is preparing for the glorification of Vladyka Juvenaly as a local saint."

8. CHINESE ORTHODOX MISSIONERIES[46]

It is hoped that, in the future, more can be known and written about the lives and activities of the Chinese Orthodox of years past. Their stories are undoubtedly preserved and told among the present Chinese Orthodox, but memories fade, witnesses go to their rest, and we are left with less information than we would like, but we must share what we do have in hope that more will be added later.

"Believing that the Lord had not led half a million emigrants from Russia to China by chance, St. John (Maximovitch) was deeply convinced that the most important task of the emigration was the preaching of Orthodoxy in pagan China. His opinion, however, was shared by only a few. Through St. John's efforts, on June 24, 1935, a Chinese Orthodox Brotherhood was formed. Its main goal was to unite native Chinese and Russian immigrants around the Orthodox Church. The activity of the Brotherhood was to serve as the beginning of an independent Orthodox Church in China. The Brotherhood was supposed to engage in the translation of Orthodox literature into Chinese, to conduct church and cultural work among the Chinese population, and to preach. St. John believed that Orthodoxy could not be the inheritance of only one people. The Lord came as the Savior of the whole world and his Word must be preached to the whole world.

"In the 1930s, the greatest efforts in evangelizing the Chinese people were made by Fr. Nicholas Leeshun I. His father, Joseph, had originally served at the Russian embassy in Peking. Interacting with Russians, Joseph came to faith in Christ and raised his son in Orthodoxy. Nicholas received his education at the school of the Mission in Peking. At nineteen years of age, he finished the first course of seminary education. After this, all his yearning was for the preaching of the Gospel in China.

---

[46] Ibid.

He was appointed a catechist, reader, and teacher at the Orthodox school. In the middle of the 1930s, his was ordained a deacon and in 1936, a priest.

"The Chinese Orthodox Brotherhood was headed by Yui Tsyatsin (Andrei Pavlovich Yui), known in Shanghai as a businessman and public figure who held important government posts. His collaborators were the lawyer Peter Chan and Fr. Ilya Wen Jichen. Meletius Shi was the Brotherhood's treasurer.

"The Russian Orthodox Church saw in the activities of the Brotherhood prospects for the deepening of mutual understanding between the Russian emigrants and the Chinese, and wholeheartedly supported the activities of the Brotherhood.

"The Brotherhood opened a Russian-Chinese school. In addition, courses in the Russian language and a night school were opened. The Brotherhood not only promoted the study of the Russian language by the Chinese, it also set as its goal the teaching of the Chinese language to the Russian emigrants.

"The Russian Ecclesiastical Mission in China did not cease its missionary activities in the 30s and 40s although this was truly difficult. Wartime circumstances (the Japanese occupied Shanghai during this time) and the suspicious attitude of the Japanese authorities towards any missionary work made progress nearly impossible. The Mission also lacked material means. Yet, the work continued.

"First of all, it was necessary to oppose the Uniates, who had formed in China a 'Russian Catholic Church.' Its influence was especially strong in Harbin, Tientsin, and Shanghai. Its goal was to make all Russian churches in China loyal to the papal throne, if possible. Those occupied with this were primarily the Basilian monastic order and the Jesuits. In order to convert the Orthodox, the Roman Catholics used many social charity programs; they founded schools and institutes and published many periodicals and other literature.

"In addition, Protestant Methodists, Baptists, and Adventists were also active. Among other Christian confessions it is worth mentioning the Old Believers. The Old Believers of the 'Austrian Agreement' in Harbin had a church and their own bishop. Despite a lack of resources and many challenges, the anti-sect missionary activity of the Mission was successful; Russian Catholics and Protestants often returned to the Orthodox fold.

"The spread of Orthodoxy among the Chinese population went slowly. Primarily, Chinese were baptized after studying in the schools of the Mission or prior to marriage with Orthodox. The Chinese priests helped a great deal. Services were often conducted in the Chinese language.

"Traditionally, charitable activity was a part of Orthodox church life. In Beijing, the Mission with its representation churches was a refuge for all in need. All the available buildings were occupied by Russians and Chinese seeking refuge. At the end of the 1930s, 130 Russians and about the same number of Chinese lived on the territory of the Mission. In the Mission schools, there were as many as 150 children from poor families. For the Orthodox Chinese, in addition to financial help, the work of the Mission provided means for healing, burial, baptisms, and marriages. If someone was in need, he could always hope for support from the Mission.

"In Tientsin, under the supervision of the rector of the Holy Virgin Protection Church of the Orthodox Brotherhood, there was a school, a hospital, a library, a nursery school, and a cemetery. In Tsingtao, there was also a church school and hospital."

These would be the foundations for the future autonomous Orthodox Church of China.

9. MIRACULOUS ORTHODOX ICONS IN CHINA

In addition to Orthodox churches, cathedrals, and saints, there have been many miraculous icons in China, several of which were manifested in the twentieth century, such as the above-mentioned self-renewing icon of Our Lady of Vladimir. Mention should be made of six other important and miraculous Orthodox icons that have played a role in Russian and Chinese history and are venerated by both peoples. They are the Saint Nicholas icon at the Harbin Railway Station, the Tabinskaya Icon the Mother of God, the Albazinskaya Icon of the Mother of God, the Xinjiang Icon of the Mother of God, the Harbin "Joy of All Who Sorrow" Icon of the Mother of God, and the "Port Arthur" Icon of the Mother of God.

The **Saint Nicholas "Elder from the Station"** icon was placed at the railway station from the moment of the railroad's construction. People prayed before the icon prior to their travels. Several cases of miraculous help from the icon to Chinese citizens were witnessed, so that the Chinese nicknamed the icon "The Elder from the Station."

Orthodox clergy standing by the miraculous icon of Saint Nicholas "The Elder from the Station" at the Harbin Railway Station.

"The Elder from the Station" was so popular among the Chinese that, in 1924, they did not allow the pro-Communist leaders of the railroad to take him away.

The Saint Nicholas icon, unfortunately, did not survive the Cultural Revolution. It was burned in 1966.

The **"Tabinskaya" Icon of the Mother of God (Friday after All Saints Sunday)** is one of the most mysterious icons in Russia, known to have suddenly appeared, vanished, and reappeared in several different places throughout its history. It is a Kazan style icon, being a close-up of the typical Hodigetria or Directress icon of the Theotokos, like the famous Kazanskaya miraculous icon, but not a copy of it.

The Tabinskaya Icon was discovered in 1597, as a certain Hierodeacon Ambrose of the Ascension Hermitage was walking by a salt spring. He heard a voice saying, "Take my icon," but, fearing deception, he ignored it. Sometime later upon passing the same spot, he heard the same command and discovered the icon.

A chapel was built over the salt spring, and later a monastery was constructed. In 1633, however, during a revolt of the Bashkirs, the monastery was destroyed and the icon was lost. In 1766, the icon was found again by three Bashkir shepherds, having manifested itself in a wonderful way. The shepherds were grazing their animals around the salt springs of Tabinsk when they suddenly saw the large icon of the Tabinskaya Mother of God upon a rock. The youngest shepherd, a teenager, not knowing the miracle of God, and having a hatred toward Christians, rushed toward the icon in order to slash it with his knife. Instead, he was suddenly blinded. He recovered his sight after he and his friends prayed to the "Russian God."

This man was then baptized, along with many other Bashkirs, and showed such repentance and devotion to the Mother of God that he always walked around barefoot in winter and summer, wearing a cassock and skufia (soft-sided, brimless hat worn by Orthodox clergy). He lived to be 130 years old and never departed from the icon, finally giving up his soul in Chelyabinsk.

During a cholera epidemic in 1854, the icon was transferred to Orenburg, and the epidemic ceased. Up until 1918, the icon was carried annually from Tabinsk to Orenburg, where it stayed for three months. It also accompanied the Orenburg Cossacks to the front lines in World War I. The Tabinskaya Icon then became the patroness of the Orenburg Cossacks.

The Tabinskaya Icon was brought to China by Methodius, Archbishop of Orenburg, and the Cossacks in the army of Ataman Dutov. When the army reached Blagoveshchensk on the Amur River, however, the icon would go no farther—it would not be moved. In grief and despair, the Russian soldiers prayed to Our Lady of Tabinsk, who had always saved them, but seemingly did not want them to go abroad. Their need was urgent as the Red Army was approaching and would soon destroy them.

Bishop Nestor (Anisimov) of Kamchatka and Archbishop Methodius of Orenberg and the other clergy with them built a chapel out of reeds over the miraculous icon. The clergy and the army prayed before the icon for three days with fasting and tears, and afterward the holy icon of Our Lady of Tabinsk moved across the border with them into China.

For a long time, the icon was at the left *kliros*[47] of the Orthodox church in Ürümqi, Xinjiang, the gateway to the Silk Road. St. Jonah (Pokrovsky) was the rector of the St. Nicholas Church before he became Bishop of Hankow. It is not clear if the icon was later moved to Harbin.

In the late 1960s, during the Cultural Revolution, the St. Nicholas Church was destroyed and the Tabinskaya Icon was lost. There are three different stories of what happened to the icon. One says that the icon escaped from China—there were many Orthodox Russian and Chinese refugees fleeing the Communists after World War II and the Cultural Revolution—and went to Australia with Archimandrite Philaret (Voznesensky), later the head of the Russian Church Abroad. From there, the icon went to the United States, ending up in San Francisco, where it disappeared.

---

[47] The *kliros* is a section of an Eastern Orthodox church dedicated to the choir. In a cruciform church, the altar is in the eastern apse and the *kliros*, if there is only one, is generally located in the south semitransept, the south-facing arm of the cruciform church. It is traditional, however, for there to be two *kliroi* for the sake of antiphonal chanting.

Another story says that the Tabinskaya Icon was confiscated by the Communist Chinese authorities and is now most likely stored somewhere at the repositories of the Chinese Ministry of Culture.

A third story, however, is told by the remaining Chinese Orthodox faithful of Yining. Though the town is around eleven hours away by train from Ürümqi, it was one of several Chinese cities in Northwest China having special veneration for the Tabinskaya Icon. These Chinese Orthodox gather in private homes to pray, their churches having been destroyed or seized. Some of the faithful have managed to rescue old icons and service books. But most, not having prayer books of their own, rely on prayers they have carefully copied out and shared. They remember where the St. Nicholas Church stood, holding the treasured icon of the Most Holy Theotokos. They do not believe the icon was destroyed in the fire that destroyed the church, but that it was concealed by one of the parishioners somewhere outside the city.

The location of the Tabinskaya Icon of the Mother of God Monastery in Russia was also ravaged by the Communists. The chapel that had housed the icon and the cave containing the salt spring where the icon was found were closed, processions were banned, and veneration of the holy icon was suppressed. The faithful would still come to the sacred spot and pray the akathist hymn to the Tabinskaya Icon, sheltered among the birch trees. Then, the authorities ambushed and arrested the faithful and cut down the trees. Brave Christians still returned and prayed by the stumps, so the authorities burned the stumps and used the site for a trash dump.

The Soviet authorities tried to turn the holy mineral spring into a treatment center, but word spread that snakes filled the baths and a mysterious woman in black was seen patrolling the chapel. As a result, the chapel and spring were blown up in 1972, but the holy waters only bubbled up in several new locations.

In 1998, with the blessing of Patriarch Alexei II, the Convent of the Tabinskaya Icon of the Mother of God was opened, and now a golden-domed church overlooks the new site. The Tabinskaya Icon of the Mother of God is celebrated on the Friday of All Saints Week, or the ninth Friday after Pascha (Easter).

The **Albazinskaya Icon of the Mother of God (March 9/22)** received its name from the Russian fort of Albazin on the Chinese border, just as the Albazin Cossacks who were captured there and taken to Peking. This is an icon "Of the Sign" or Znameny. It depicts the Word made flesh inside his mother, in reference to Isaiah 7:14,[48] and is sometimes referred to as the "Word Made Flesh" Icon.

In 1665, when the Russians returned to Albazin after the war with China that led to the establishment of the Russian-Chinese Albazinian community in Peking, Archimandrite Hermogenes of the Kirensk Holy Trinity Monastery came to Albazin bringing the icon of the Mother of God "The Word Was Made Flesh." In 1671, Fr. Hermogenes founded a monastery in Bosyanoi, which became the icon's home. In 1681, a local Sobor (Council) of the Russian Church resolved to send missionaries to the areas of the Lena and Amur Rivers to spread the Christian faith among the local Tungusic population. This mission bore much fruit.

In 1685, the Chinese again marched on Albazin with an army 15,000 strong and encircled the fortress. Inside were 450 Russian soldiers with only three cannons. The first assault was repulsed. Then, the Chinese piled up firewood and kindling against the wooden walls of the fortress and set it ablaze. The Russians were forced to abandon the fortress, but the Mother of God did not abandon her chosen city. Scouts reported that the Chinese had suddenly and hurriedly withdrawn from Albazin, even ignoring the Chinese Emperor's order to destroy the crops growing in the surrounding fields. This miraculous intervention of the Mother of God not only ousted the enemy from Russian territory, but even preserved the Russians' daily bread.

---

[48] "Therefore the Lord himself will give you a sign: behold, the virgin shall conceive and bear a Son, and shall call his name Immanuel."

The fortress would be under siege three times again the following year. During one such siege, the Chinese rained down a hail of fiery arrows and red hot cannon balls. There was so much smoke that neither the city nor its defenders could be seen. But the city did not fall. In December, acknowledging defeat, the Chinese lifted the siege. Of the 826 Russian defenders of Albazin, only 150 men survived. The Russian survivors fled with the icon to Sretensk and contributed further to the spread of Christianity in the Far East.

In 1868, Bishop Benjamin of Kamchatka, the successor of St. Innocent Veniaminov, moved the Albazinskaya Icon to Blagoveshchensk, the new capital of the Amur Region. In 1900, during the Boxer Rebellion, Chinese troops suddenly appeared on the Chinese bank of the Amur, across from Blagoveshchensk. For nineteen days, the enemy rained down artillery fire on the undefended city. The river was shallow and the region faced the threat of invasion. The Orthodox people took refuge inside the Church of the Annunciation and prayed before the Albazinskaya Icon without interruption for the length of the siege, and their hope in the Most Holy Theotokos was not put to shame. The Chinese themselves later reported seeing throughout the siege above the city a radiant woman who instilled fear in their hearts as she cast aside the missiles they fired. Through the prayers of the Mother of God, the enemy was warded off. Thus, the Albazinskaya Icon has been regarded as the defender of the Russian Far East. Many miracles and healings since then have taken place through the icon, which is also well known for help in times of pregnancy and childbirth.

In 1924, the Church of the Annunciation was burned down and the icon was moved to the St. Elias Chapel. From 1938 on, the Albazinskaya Icon was a museum exhibit.

In 1991, when the icon returned in procession to the Church of the Annunciation in Blagoveshchensk, it was reported that, despite the bitter cold, all the flowers adorning the image of the Mother of God remained alive and that tears were streaming from the Virgin's eyes.[49] The feast day of the Albazinskaya Icon of the Mother of God is March 9/22.

---

[49] http://russights.ru/post_1291482133.html

The **Xinjiang Icon of the Mother of God** also came to China with the White Russian refugees and was installed in a village church in Yining, Xinjiang province. Upset by the construction of the church, a group of local Muslim Uighurs entered the church and the imam stabbed the icon on the face with a knife. The face of the Mother of God then began to bleed. The terrified imam ran out of the church with the others close behind. Later, there were many other miracles associated with the icon, one of which was that the wound on the face of the icon healed by itself. This icon remained in the church until the Cultural Revolution, when it was seized by Red Guards and thrown into a fire. Eyewitnesses reported that the icon was not burnt, but simply disappeared into the flames. According to local tradition, when Orthodoxy is reestablished in Xinjiang and people are free, the icon will reappear.

--Information on the Tabinskaya, Albazinskaya, and Xingjiang Icons of the Mother of God from: www.orthodox.cn/index-en.html

The **Icon of the Mother of God "Joy of All Who Sorrow"** has a special place in the history of Orthodox China. It is the patroness of the San Francisco cathedral built by St. John the Wonderworker. The icon also symbolized poignantly the experience both of the exiled Russian community and of the Orthodox Chinese, who kept their faith in the midst of deprivation and persecution.

The **Harbin "Joy of All Who Sorrow" Icon of the Mother of God** is another miraculously self-renewing icon which appeared at the vital and blessed junction of love for God and love for people.

In the 1920s, in the city of Harbin, a young Bishop Nestor (Anisimov), labored to build a "House of Mercy," a charitable institution that served as a hostel for the elderly and sick and an orphanage for children. He consecrated a church at the House of Mercy in honor of the "Joy of All Who Sorrow" Icon of the Mother of God. One of the bishop's close assistants, a very pious Russian lady, Ekaterina Ivanovna Kurmey, donated her own "Joy of All Who Sorrow" icon for use in the House of Mercy church. This was an ancient icon, already darkened so much from time that it was almost impossible to discern the faces of the Lord Jesus Christ and the Most Holy Theotokos, let alone read the inscriptions.

One day, the rector of the church, Father Julian Sumnevich, who was particularly revered by the Orthodox residents of Harbin for his spirituality and irreproachable life, noticed that the old icon was beginning to renew itself. Not believing his own eyes, Fr. Julian decided to wait awhile and see what would happen. But the renewal was progressing quickly, and in a few hours the icon was so bright that the miracle was undoubtable. By the next day, the holy icon was like new—the colors were bright and the faces were clear and distinct.

This working of God's grace inspired the whole city, and is still remembered. Orthodox believers from all over China came to Harbin to venerate the miraculously renewed icon, which became one of the most important holy objects in the city.

The last rector of the church in the House of Mercy was Archimandrite **Philaret (Voznesensky) (+November 8/21, 1985)**, who would later become a metropolitan and the third First-Hierarch of the Russian Orthodox Church Outside of Russia. (His relics, which repose in Holy Trinity Monastery in Jordanville, New York, are incorrupt, and he is venerated by many Orthodox for his sanctity and confession of the faith.)

When Fr. Philaret left Harbin for Australia after great difficulty, and then continued on to the United States, the renewed Harbin "Joy of All Who Sorrow" Icon of the Mother of God remained in the House of Mercy church, along with other holy objects. With the departure of its last rector, the church was closed, and its holy objects and items became the property of the Chinese government.

It was only with much effort and difficulty that the acting warden of the church, Z. L. Tauz-Zvereva, managed to obtain permission from the authorities to export the holy icon. In the fall of 1965, during Metropolitan Philaret's trip to Europe, the renewed Harbin "Joy of All Who Sorrow" Icon of the Mother of God arrived at the Synodal Cathedral of the Russian Church Abroad in New York, where it was placed in the lower Church of St. Sergius of Radonezh. The cathedral clergy have testified that, on occasion, holy myrrh will appear on the surface of the icon.

Metropolitan Philaret once gave a sermon on the renewal of the Harbin "Joy of All Who Sorrow" Icon in which he said:
"Russia has been at Calvary, and the Russian Church on the Cross! In order to encourage and comfort the believers, the Lord has sent a miraculous sign, which is not known by our ancestors. In Russia has begun a renewal of the icons; when old, very faded icons have suddenly started to shine with light, as if they just had been painted. It started from there, and then the wave came around to us, to the Far East. And there, in the city of Harbin, I remember how happily excited was Russian Orthodox Harbin (and there were 75,000 Orthodox people at one time - the whole city), how Russian Orthodox people were excited about that amazing miracle that happened.

"The House of Mercy was in need, it was difficult at first. And then a miracle happened. This icon, in front of which we are now praying, was then a blackboard: it was impossible to tell what was on it. Neither the sacred figures nor the inscriptions were perceptible. It was a black, sooty, oily board and nothing else. Yet, in the course of one day, this icon was renewed and shone like new! Now, as you can see, you can decipher everything on it, and many decades have gone by since. After this, all of Russian Orthodox Harbin had recourse to this icon, and the image of the Mother of God Joy of All Who Sorrow was one of the greatest and holiest relics in our favorite city of Harbin. There have undoubtedly been phenomena of the marvelous grace of God related to this icon. One girl was dying, hopelessly ill, and she was completely healed and recovered. One man lost the most necessary documents for travel and there was no possible human way to find them again. But he prayed to the Mother of God, and she came to the rescue, for that which was lost was found unexpectedly.

"This image is called the Mother of God 'Joy of All Who Sorrow.' There are enough sorrows at the present time. Everyone has them, and blessed is he who in faith appeals to her, the Joy of All Who Sorrow, the Mother of God, for she will certainly hear our prayer."

The **Port Arthur Icon of the Mother of God (May 13/26 and August 16/29)** is rather unique among miraculous icons because of the tragic story surrounding it. In 1898, China leased Lyushun (also known as Port Arthur), a port northwest of the Korean Peninsula, to Russia as a buffer against Japan. In this way, Russia became a protector of China from Japanese designs. Port Arthur, since it was an ice-free harbor, became a port for Russia's Pacific Fleet.

In December 1903, the Most Holy Theotokos appeared to an old Russian sailor and Crimean War veteran in Kiev. She was surrounded by angels and holding the icon of the Savior "Not Made By Hands." She told the sailor, "Russia will soon be involved in a very difficult war. Paint an icon showing my appearance as it is now and send it to Port Arthur. If the icon is in that city, Orthodoxy will triumph over paganism and Russian warriors will attain my help, my patronage, and their victory."

The old sailor did exactly as he was commanded and the Port Arthur Icon of the "Victory of the Theotokos" was painted in Kiev. When the Russo-Japanese War broke out in 1904, the icon was entrusted to an admiral to be sent to Port Arthur. However, that admiral procrastinated and the next admiral entrusted with the icon simply forgot about it.

73

Finally, after protests from common people and the Imperial Family, the icon was taken to Vladivostok, for by that time Port Arthur was already under siege by the Japanese. A courageous veteran named Nikolai Fyodorov sought to take the icon to Port Arthur even at the cost of his own life, but the ship he would have sailed on was delayed by inclement weather. Meanwhile, Port Arthur fell and Russia gave up the war, even though, had Russia pressed on, Japan would have capitulated instead. As a result, Russia lost both Port Arthur and half of Sakhalin Island.

After the Bolshevik Revolution, the church in which the icon was kept in Vladivostok was destroyed and the icon was lost until 1998, when pilgrims from Vladivostok happened to visit Jerusalem. There, in an antique shop close to the Church of the Holy Sepulcher, they found the original icon. It was brought back to Vladivostok, and since then, the original and copies of it have worked miracles, being venerated in Russia, Canada, America, China, and in Port Arthur itself, now Lyushunkou District, nearly 100 years after it was supposed to have arrived.

Thus, the Port Arthur Icon of the "Victory of the Theotokos" can truly be said to be a Chinese icon, though it was made in Russia.

+ + + + + + +

After the Communist takeover of China in 1949, "Russian Atlantis" submerged into historical memory. Yet, this short period was formative for both the Russian Orthodox diaspora and the native Chinese Orthodox. It was a healing balm over the wounds of the Boxer Rebellion and illumined the great potential for a lasting and growing Orthodox Christian presence in China. Though it was a flash of brilliant light lasting only a moment, the memory of that light could not be extinguished in the darkness that followed. It survived in the monuments left behind—churches, icons, saints, and even stories. It survived in pictures and photographs in historical archives and family albums of its descendants who now live in all parts of the world. It lives in the heart, the place from whence it came.

Orthodox clergy and members of the Theology School of the St. Vadimir Institute by the walls of St. Sofia Cathedral in Harbin in 1939. [50]

(1) N. Makarov; (2) Nikolay Gondati; (3) Evgeny Sumarokov; (4) Archpriest Nikolay Trufanov; (5) Archpriest Aristarkh Ponomarev; (6) Archimandrite Nafanail (Porshev); (7) Archbishop Dimitri (Voznesenski); (8) Metropolitan Meleti (Zaborovsky); (9) Protopresviter Mikhail (Filologov); (10) Iraida Chistyakova; (11), Archpriest Victor (Guriev); (12) Stepan Babich; (13) Alexander Khavaev; (14) Mitrofan Vtorov; (15) Archpriest Nikolay (Kushkov); (16) Archpriest Alexander (Chistiakov);

---

[50] The School was opened September 9, 1934, with two graduation classes in 1937 and 1939. The photograph and names were submitted by T.V. Pavlovich (Marianova), M Khripko and V. Rudenko.

(17) Archpriest Dimitri (Lavrov); (18) Hippolite Raisky; (20) Archpriest Ioann (Zaerko); (21) Archpriest Georgy (Chernavin); (22) Alexander Pershin; (23) Archpriest Innocent (Petelin); (25) Kiryll Zaitsev (Archimandrite Konstantin); (26) N. Zakhvatov; (28) Ioann Vorotnikov; (29) Archpriest Victor (Chernykh); (31) Archpriest Mikhail (Andreev); (32) Archpriest Simeon (Novosiltsev); (33) Archpriest Nikolay (Kiklovich); (34) Archpriest Ioann (Kliarovich); (37) Nikolay Deputatov; (38) Fedor Turchaninov; (39) Ivan Popov; (42) Archpriest Nikolay (Mukhin); (44) Archpriest Nikolay (Lukin); (45) Archpriest Vladimir (Petrov); (46) Archpriest Mikhail (Pakhomov); (49) Archpriest Faddei (Siniy); (51) Archpriest Simeon (Dzugaev); (52) Nikolay Nepovetov; (53) Ivan Kostiuchik; (54) Priest Nikolay (Shesterov); (55) A. Nadtochey; (56) Boris Starikhin; (57) Archdeacon Prokopy (Makoveev); (59) Archpriest Nikolay (Ponomarev); (61) Archimandrite Georgy (Shatilov); (63) Archimandrite Innocent (Melnikov); (64) Archpriest Sergey (Lebedev); (65) Priest Ilya (Novokreshchenykh); (66) Porfiry Arkhipov; (68) Archdeacon Nikolay (Vertmitsky); (70) Vladimir Inoevs; (71) Archdeacon Simeon (Korostylev).

After 1954, most of the Orthodox clergy left Harbin and settled in different parts of the world. Some of them returned to Soviet Union, while others moved to Australia, Brazil or United States. In 1963, there were only two Russian priests left in Harbin – Fr. Nikolai Starikov and Protopresbyter Victor Chernykh. Fr Nikolai left for Australia in March of 1963 and Protopresbyter Victor remained the last Russian priest in Harbin before his final move to France in 1965.

Protopresbyter Victor Chernykh (1887-1967), the last Russian Orthodox priest of Harbin (passport photo of 1965).

Protopresbyter Victor Chernykh serves Panikhida for the Russian soldiers who died in the war of 1904-1905. Harbin, 1960.

10. THE AUTONOMOUS CHINESE ORTHODOX CHURCH

In 1950, Archbishop Victor (Svyatin) wrote to Patriarch Alexei I (Simansky) of Moscow about the necessity of broadening missionary work in the Beijing Diocese. The patriarch was well informed about the recent changes in Chinese politics.

Therefore the patriarch required Archbishop Victor, over the next ten years, with God's help, to establish a Chinese Orthodox Church with Chinese bishops, Chinese priests, Chinese monks and nuns, Chinese missionaries, and most importantly, with Chinese parishioners [30]. As it turned out, there were only six years to do this.

Chinese and Russian clergy.

In 1950, following the patriarchal request, Archbishop Victor had already ordained five Chinese priests and four deacons [34, p.154]. That same year, in the Holy Trinity Lavra near Moscow, the first Chinese bishop, Simeon Du (1885-1965, from the Dubininy family of Albazinians) was consecrated. In 1952, he established a theological school in Shanghai.

Bishop Simeon (Du) of Shanghai (1885-1965), first Chinese Orthodox bishop.

In 1957, with the permission of the Communist leaders of China, the second Chinese bishop Vasily (Yao, 1888-1962) was consecrated and sent as a bishop to Beijing. He was a humble man and it took a long time to convince him to accept the position of bishop. The State Soviet of the People's Republic of China Department of Religion agreed to make the Bishop of Beijing head of the Autonomous Chinese Orthodox Church.

Bishop Vasily (Yao) of Peking and China (1888-1962), head of the Autonomous Chinese Orthodox Church

Upon returning to China, Bishop Vasily was supposed to become, according to canonical norms, the head of the Chinese Orthodox Church. Such a decision was to be made during a Chinese Orthodox All-Church Council. However, Bishop Simeon opposed this council, and this split the Chinese clergy into two camps. The ambitions of the first Chinese bishop and the progressively worsening political situation inside the country made the process of firmly establishing the Autonomous Chinese Orthodox Church impossible to complete before the whirlwind of the Cultural Revolution.

Destruction of Orthodox churches in China during the Cultural Revolution

During the Chinese Cultural Revolution, from 1966 to 1976, most of the Orthodox churches in China were destroyed, demolished, or disfigured and used for entertainment or commercial purposes. The destruction took place in many Chinese cities, but in Harbin alone it involved the following:

In 1958, the Holy Annunciation Cathedral in Harbin was closed and used as a circus school. In 1970, the cathedral was demolished. Holy Assumption Church in Harbin was turned into entertainment room with disfiguring mirrors for a "laughing room," which exists there still. Other churches were confiscated by the state powers and used for commercial and utility purposes. Two Orthodox cemeteries with nearly 100,000 graves were destroyed. In 1965, the last Orthodox monastery in Harbin was closed, and its last nun and Mother Superior Ariadna left for the United States. In 1966, the Saint Nicholas Cathedral in Harbin was demolished.

In Shanghai, the Saint Nicholas Church was not touched only because someone came up with an idea to decorate the church facade with Mao Zedong's portrait.

In 1965, after the death of Bishop Simeon (Du), the main cathedral of Shanghai was closed. In the years following, it has been used as a storage place, a restaurant, a stock exchange, and a night club.

Demolition of the Saint Nicholas Cathedral in Harbin, 1966.

The conditions under which the Orthodox Church existed in China at this time were tragic. One of the parishioners of the Harbin Diocese wrote: "Our priests have been captured; they were dragged through the city streets with tall, humiliating hats on their heads bearing revolutionary slogans. All our churches are demolished; the cathedral has been destroyed completely, and in its place a revolutionary monument will be erected" [34, p.188].

Many priests, after being publicly mocked, were tried, convicted, and sentenced to compulsory labor in mines and quarries. One of the most tragic stories is the humiliation of Protopresbyter Stefan U, a priest of Saint Alexei Church in Modyagow.

"In front of his church, a low table with sharp stones was erected, and Father Stefan was pushed to his knees and onto the stones. He was mockingly dressed in fool's robes, his head adorned by fool's hat that was filled with sharp scrap metal, and his face was painted with soot. For two days, he was beaten by wooden mallets on his head and struck with a metal rod on his shoulder. His cross was spat upon. Being half-dead, he was transported into a prison hospital where, following a minimal recovery, he was later shot to death. The relics of this new martyr now rest at the Orthodox cemetery of Sankeshu near Harbin" [30].

Until the death of Mao Zedong, in the People's Republic of China it was unthinkable to talk about religion in public. Chinese Orthodox in Shanghai "kept their icons in closets, hidden behind clothes" [25].

Later, following the early stages of Deng Xiaoping's reforms, Catholics and Protestants in China were able to organize forums in 1980, where they confirmed their patriotic course established before the Cultural Revolution. At the time, however, the autonomous Chinese Orthodox Church did not have the same potential for revival in the country, for the clergy were all but wiped out.

11. ORTHODOXY IN CHINA TODAY

The contemporary Orthodox community in China consists of around 15,000 parishioners, though they are not united in one religious organization. Most of them live in Xinjiang, Inner Mongolia, the northeastern province of Heilongjiang, and also in Beijing (Peking) and Shanghai [34, p.196]. In the entire country, there are currently four Orthodox churches,[51] including the Church of the Intercession in Harbin; the Church of Saint Innocent of Irkutsk in Ergun (Labdarin, Inner Mongolia), consecrated in 2009; Saint Nicholas Church in Kuldgi (Inin), consecrated in 2003; and Saint Nicholas Church in Ürümqi, restored in 1991 by the Chinese authorities. The most well-known among them is the Church of Holy Protection in Harbin, which was re-opened in 1986. However,

The Church of Saint Innocent of Irkutsk in Ergun (Labdarin, Inner Mongolia).

---

[51] There is also the Saint Innocent Church in the Russian Consulate in Peking and the Assumption Orthodox Church, which was restored in 2009. In addition, there is a parish in the Russian Consulate in Shanghai. These churches belong to the Moscow Patriarchate, and they have official priests. However, these churches are not accessible to ordinary Chinese parishioners

Saint Nicholas Church in Kuldgi (Inin) (left). Saint Nicholas Church in Ürümqi (Dimtzya –Uighur Autonomous Region) (right).

Church of Intersession of the Theotokos in Harbin.

there is not even one priest in all of these churches!

This happened because, according to Orthodox canon law, only a bishop can ordain a priest. And both Orthodox bishops of the autonomous Orthodox Church of China are now deceased. Bishop Simeon (Du) died in 1965, and Bishop Vasily (Yao) died in 1962, without consecrating a new bishop and leaving a successor. (According to Orthodox canon law, the consecration of a bishop requires at least two bishops.) Thus, apostolic succession in the autonomous Orthodox Church of China has been interrupted.

The Last Clergy of the Autonomous Church of China

Among a few clergy of the autonomous Church of China who survived by the beginning of the new millennium are Priest Michael Van Tzyuashen (b.1924) and Protodeacon Evangel Lu, who have now retired and currently live in Shanghai.[52]

Protopresbyter Michael Li (b.1925) was a victim of political repression and sentenced to compulsive labor in quarries from 1966 to 1984. Later, he served as a priest in Shanghai and then immigrated to Australia where now he serves as a priest for the Russian Church Abroad in the Orthodox Chinese community of Sydney [11].

Priest Gregory Tzhu (1924-2000) served at the Church of Sts. Boris and Gleb in Chenkhe and in the church at Moscow military headquarters [34, p.192]. During the Cultural Revolution, he was mocked and dragged through the city, forced to carry a humiliating poster saying: "He is kissing Khrushchev's feet"[15]. He was the last priest officially recognized by the ruling powers. (It is possible that Chinese Orthodox were persecuted more particularly than those of other confessions because of their connection to Russia and the Communist Chinese government's antagonism toward the Soviet Union.)

Protopresbyter Ilya Wen (1896-2007) lived for 110 years. He was the rector of the Main Cathedral of the "Surety of Sinners" Icon of the Mother of God in Shanghai. Later, he emigrated first to Hong Kong, where he started the Holy Resurrection Parish, and then to San Francisco, where he served at the Holy Virgin - Joy of all Who Sorrow Cathedral.

Archpriest Alexander Du (1923-2003) served as a priest first at several churches in Beijing, and after the Cultural Revolution continued serving at local homes.

According to Chinese law, religious organizations in the country exist according to a principle of three-way self-sufficiency including "self-ruling, self-financing and self-dissemination." Such a principle was used as a foundation for the laws regarding religious organizations in the 1950s [31]. The latter means that foreign missionaries cannot give sermons, and foreign priests cannot serve without permission from the Chinese authorities. For

---

[52] As of 2013.

example, the official Catholic Church in China exists as independent of the Vatican since, according to the law, it cannot be ruled by a foreign religious center. The Catholic Church that is ruled by the Vatican also exists in China, but illegally. At the same time, the official Chinese Catholic Church has enough bishops making it sufficient to ordain new priests (according to the Roman Catholic rules, three bishops have to participate in a priest's ordination). Back in 1926, the Vatican had consecrated six Chinese bishops.

During last twenty years, several Orthodox Chinese studied at the theological seminaries of Moscow and St. Petersburg. Two of them, including Reader Papyi Fu, completed theological training, but were not allowed to serve as priests by the Chinese authorities.

Now the Chinese Department of Religious Affairs has approved two candidates from the Holy Protection Church in Harbin to study in the Russian Orthodox seminaries to prepare for the priesthood. In 2012, Alexander Yui and Vasily U were sent to study in the Orthodox seminaries of Moscow and St. Petersburg.

Among other developments, the restoration of two Orthodox churches destroyed during the Cultural Revolution should also be mentioned. The churches were restored by the Chinese authorities in places having a high-density Russian diaspora population. This reflects the status of Orthodoxy in China as a religion of a national minority.

In addition, in 2009, at the recreational center "Volga Estate" near Harbin, a local Chinese developer built an exact copy of the Saint Nicholas Church in Harbin. It is now used as a museum.

A special place in the Orthodox life of China belongs to the Parish of Peter and Paul in Hong Kong. The parish was organized in 2003, under the Archpriest Denis Pozdnayev. The law of Hong Kong does not restrict religious life to the same degree as mainland China. Therefore, the parish makes its main goal to enrich the intellectual life of the Chinese Orthodox by focusing on publishing books, brochures, and theological works in hopes of later attracting new Orthodox converts. The parish also collaborates with the Institute of Chinese-Christian Relations in Hong Kong. The publishing house is financed by private donations. Currently, by their efforts, over twenty books have been translated into Chinese, including Fr. George Florovsky's "Ways of Russian Theology" and "Elder Silouan," by Archimandrite Sofrony. Researchers of the rich tradition of mysticism in China believe that such a tradition is capable of being synthesized with Byzantine theology and that such a synthesis may lay the

foundation for a unique Chinese theology. Although there are only a few Chinese citizens of Hong Kong among parishioners of the Sts. Peter and Paul Church, every year Father Denis baptizes several Chinese in mainland China. There are also two Greek Orthodox churches in Hong Kong and Taiwan under the Ecumenical Patriarch of Constantinople.

Archpriest Denis Pozdnayev, the rector of the Parish of Sts. Peter and Paul in Hong Kong (Russian Orthodox Church).

Patriarch Kirill's visit to China from May 10-15 2013 was an important event in lives of the Chinese Orthodox. His Holiness served Holy Liturgies in Beijing, Shanghai, and Harbin, and met with Xi Jinping, which was the first official meeting of China's leader with the head of a Christian Church. Some of the positive outcomes of the Patriarchal visit lay in achieving a mutual understanding that the lack of priests in China is an abnormal situation for the autonomous Chinese Orthodox Church and in reaching an official agreement about Chinese students to study in Russian Orthodox seminaries. Metropolitan Hilarion (Alfeyev), who also participated in the visit, further commented on the issue: "The problem is that the Chinese leadership believes only people who were vetted by the State Committee on Religious Affairs may go to the seminary and be ordained as priests in China. However, we will be working with the Chinese side on this issue and will continue until we get priests assigned to serve in active churches in the People's Republic of China."

On December 9, 2014, another important event took place as an Orthodox deacon of Chinese origin Anatoly Coon (Coon Cheun Min) was elevated to a priesthood at the Cathedral of St. Innocent of Irkutsk in Khabarovsk by His Eminence

Metropolitan Ignatius of Khabarovsk and Amur. An ordination took place on St. Innocent's feast day and it was the first ordination of Orthodox priest of the Chinese origin for the last sixty years. Newly ordained Fr. Anatoly was sent to serve in the parish of Sts. Peter and Paul in Hong Kong and to participate in missionary work among the Chinese population of Hong Kong and continental China.

What else did Orthodoxy give to China?

Chinese Orthodoxy is not large enough for us to speak easily about its specific influence outside of the Russian or general Christian context. Nevertheless, in addition to education and charity, which were the main part of Orthodox missionary work, music and particularly architecture should be mentioned. Saint Sofia Cathedral has now became a symbol of Harbin. This is not just a historical fact, but also a recognition of the grandeur of Orthodox architecture.

Chzhan Suichzhu wrote in his monumental work "Orthodoxy and Orthodoxy in China": "Chinese culture was significantly enriched due to interactions with Christian culture and because of the diversified cultures of foreign Christian missionaries" [42, p.345].

One of the important influences of Orthodoxy in the context of general Christianity is marital monogamy, which was established in China through contact with Western civilization and Christian influence.

In the area of science, the theistic principle of the Christian religion in separating the Creator from creation has stimulated experimental activity, desacralized nature, and provoked interest in the particular and concrete.

In the field of social anthropology, Christianity enhanced individuality and increased the role of individual personality that, in the traditional Chinese mind, was almost completely dissolved in a collective.

"In a new situation, Christianity was able to give answers to fundamental questions of existence for many Chinese intellectuals more so than Taoism or Buddhism" [32].

APPENDIX I. ORTHODOX SPIRITUAL MISSIONS IN CHINA[53]

Mission	Years	Head of the Mission
First	1715-1728	Hilarion (Lezhaisky), Archimandrite (1657-1717)
Second	1729-1735	Antony (Platkovsky), Archimandrite (d. 1746)
Third	1736-1743	Hilarion (Trusov), Archimandrite (d. 1741)
Forth	1744-1755	Gervasy (Lintsevsky), Archimandrite (d. 1769)
Fifth	1755-1771	Amvrosy (Yumatov), Archimandrite (d. 1771)
Sixth	1771-1781	Nickolay (Tsvet), Archimandrite (d. 1784)
Seventh	1781-1794	Joakim (Shishkovsky), Archimandrite (d. 1795)
Eigth	1794-1807	Sophrony (Gribovsky), Archimandrite (d. 1814)
Nineth	1807-1821	Ioakinf (Bichurin), Archimandrite (1777-1853)
Tenth	1821-1830	Peter (Kamensky), Archimandrite (1765-1845)
Eleventh	1830-1840	Veniamin (Morachevich), Archimandrite
Twelveth	1840-1849	Polikarp (Tugarinov), Archimandrite
Thirteenth	1850-1858	Pallady (Kafarov), Archimandrite
Fourteenth	1858-1864	St. Gury (Karpov), Archimandrite
Fifteenth	1865-1878	Pallady (Kafarov), Archimandrite
Sixteenth	1879-1883	Flavian (Gorodetsky), Archimandrite
Sevneteenth	1884-1896	Amphilokhy (Lutovinov), Archimandrite
Eighteenth	1896-1931	Innocent (Figurovsky), Bishop
Nineteenth	1931-1933	Simon (Vinogradov), Bishop
Twentieth	1933-1956	Victor (Svyatin), Metropolitan

---

[53] Based on: Titarenko M.L. "Orthodoxy in China" – Moscow, 2010 and Datsyshen V.G. "History of the Russian Spiritual Mission in China" – Hong Kong, 2010.

Appendix II. Map of Orthodox Churches in China

Map of the Orthodox churches in China. (Compiled by G.S. Bondareva)

Location	Construction (-destruction) year	Church/parish name
1. Ang'angxi	1900	St. Peter and St. Paul Church
2. Anda	1900	St. Nicholas and St. Alexis Church
3. Aomen (Macau)	1934	Holy Trinity Family Church
4. Barim	1937	St. Sergius Church
5. Bukhedu	1902	St. Alexandra Church
6. Beidaihe	1905	Church (?)
7. Beidaihe	1900	St. John the Baptist Church
8. The Western Hills (Western Beijing)	1910	Elevation of the Holy Cross Church
9. Wafangdian	1905	Church (?)
10. Weihuifu (Henan Province)	1900	Church and School
11. Hong Kong	1934	St. Peter and St. Paul Church
12. Guangzhou	1934	Our Lady Unexpected Joy, Home Church
13. Gongzhuling	1907	Church
14. Dalian	1901	The Entry of the Theotokos Church
15. Dalian	ca 1900	Church in Nun's Monastery in Xiajiahezi
16. Dalian	ca 1900	Archangel Michael Church
17. Dalian	ca 1900	Chapel-Church, Russian military cemetery
18. Dong Ting Village (~50 miles of Peking)	1899-1900	St. Innocent of Irkutsk Church
19. Dong Ting Village	1902	St. John the Apostle Church
20. Imjanpo	1901	St. Sergius Church
21. Yingkou	1906	Church (?)
22. Yichun	1920	Dormition of the Theotokos Church
23. Zhangjiakou (Kalgan)	1899	Holy Trinity Church
24. Ghulja (Yining)	2000	St. Nicholas Church
25. Ghulja (Yining)	1872	St. Elijah Church
26. Ghulja (Yining	ca 1900	St. Nicholas Church
27. Ghulja (Yining)	1937	Our Lady of Tabynsk Church
28. Lamadian	ca 1900	Gospel Hall
29. Lüshun City (Port Arthur)	ca 1900	St. Vladimir Chapel at the cemetery
30. Liaoyang	1904	Church
31. Manila (the Republic of Philippines)	1934	Home Church of Our Lady of Iviron
32. Manchuria	1937	Monastery Our Lady of Vladimir in Sun Valley
33. Manchuria	1900-1980	St. Innocent Church
34. Manchuria	1903	St. Seraphim Church
35. Mukden (Shenyang)	1900	Chapel, Russian military cemetery
36. Mianduhe	1911	St. Vladimir (St. Nicholas) Church
37. Naidzhin-Bulak	1937	St. Nicholas Church
38. Beijing	1902-1957	Church of All Holy Martyrs
39. Beijing	1901	St. Innocent of Irkutsk

90

40. Beijing	1903 - 1986	St. Seraphim of Sarov
41. Beijing	1729 - 1991	The Meeting of the Lord
42. Beijing	1732	Holy Dormition Church and Bell Tower at the Russian Mission
43. Beijing	1696 - 1730	St. Sophia (the Holy Wisdom) Chapel
44. Pogranichnaya station (Suifenhe)	1915	Stone church - replacing the church burned down in 1909
45. Pogranichnaya	1901	St. Nicholas Church
46. Tieling	1903	Church
47. Tianjin	1903	Protection of the Theotokos
48. Tianjin	1903	St. Nicholas Church
49. Ürümqi	1991	St. Nicholas Church
50. Ürümqi	ca 1900	Church at the Russian Consulate
51. Fularji 51	ca 1900	Church of The Entrance of the Theotokos into the Temple
52. Hailar	1902	Holy Transfiguration Church
53. Arxan	1900	St. Nicholas Chapel
54. Hankou (Wuhan, Hubei province)	1884	St. Alexander Nevsky
55. Harbin	1995	St. John the Baptist Church
56. Harbin	1902 - 1970	The Holy Annunciation Church
57. Harbin	ca 1900	St. Boris and St. Gleb Church
58. Harbin	1922	Our Lady of Vladimir at Nuns Monastery
59. Harbin	1933 - 1962	Iviron Chapel near St. Nicholas Cathedral
60. Harbin	ca 1900	St. John the Baptist Church near Moscow barracks
61. Harbin	1922	Monastery and Church of Our Lady of Kazan (Gondatevka)
62. Harbin	1899 - 1966	St. Nicholas Church
63. Harbin	1898	St. Nicholas Church
64. Harbin	1922	Protection of the Theotokos Church
65. Harbin	ca 1900	St. Elijah Church
66. Harbin	1912	St. Alexius Church
67. Harbin	1908	Iviron Church
68. Harbin	1921	Joy of All Who Sorrow Church
69. Harbin	1932	Holy Wisdom Church
70. Harbin	1904	Dormition of the Theotokos Church
71. Harbin	ca 1900	Church of the Holy Transfiguration
72. Harbin	1923	Church of St. John the Apostle
73. Harbin	ca 1900	Church St. Peter and St. Paul
74. Xing'an (Hinggann)	1937	St. Panteleimon (later - St. Nicholas Church) at Manchuria station
75. Hengdaohezi (Heilongjiang province)	1903	The Entry of the Theotokos into the Temple Church
76. Qingdao	1939 - 1956	St. Sophia Church

77. Qiqihar	1903	St. Peter and St. Paul Church
78. Changchun	1903	St. Nicholas Church
79. Zhalainuoer	ca 1900	Church of the Archangel Michael
80. Zhalainuoer	ca 1900	Church of the Prophet Elijah
81. Zhalantun	ca 1900	St. Nicholas Church
82. Tacheng (Chöchek)	ca 1900	Church under Russian Consulate
83. Shanghai	ca 1920	The Annunciation Church
84. Shanghai	1905	Church of the Theophany
85. Shanghai	1934	Cathedral of "The Surety of Sinners"
86. Shanghai	ca 1900	Church and shelter for elderly women
87. Shanghai	1900	Nuns Monastery Church
88. Shanghai	1934	St. Nicholas Church
89. Shanghai	1900 - 1942	St. Gabriel Church
90. Shenzhen	1900	Parish of St. Sergius of Radonezh
91. Shuachengu	1904	Church
92. Enhe	ca 1900	Church
93. Ergun	1990	St. Innocent of Irkutsk
(Labudalin, inner Mongolia)		
94. Ertsentsiantsi	1900	Our Lady of Kazan Church
95. Yakeshi	ca 1900	Our Lady of Kazan Church
96. Hong Kong		Church of St. Apostle Luke
		(Patriarchate of Constantinople)
97. Taipei (Taiwan)		Church of St. Apostle Luke
		(Patriarchate of Constantinople)

APPENDIX III. HYMNS TO CHINESE ORTHODOX SAINTS

The Holy Martyrs of the Boxer Rebellion (June 11/24)

Troparion, Tone 4 - Thy two hundred and twenty-two martyrs who shone forth in the empire of China held the Christian faith as a shield and did not bow down to idols. They accepted torture and death from their irrational countrymen and the lips of the passion-bearing youth cried: We consider as nothing suffering for Christ. We desire to obtain eternal life in exchange for this transitory life.

Troparion, Tone 3 (Today the Virgin cometh) - Let us the flock of Christ with faith and love now glorify with hymns the faithful martyrs who suffered for Christ in China. For having confessed the faith, they all went bravely unto death, not considering suffering for Christ's sake too hard to endure; but rather viewing death as a passage to a place of blessed repose. Therefore to the martyrs we cry out: remember us all, who sing your praises.

Troparion, Tone 5 - In a pagan land ye were enlightened by the Orthodox faith, and having lived in the faith but a little time, ye inherited the eternal kingdom. By the purity of your Christian ways ye put to shame the false Confucian piety and trampled demon-inspired Buddhism underfoot as refuse, sanctifying the Chinese land with your blood. Wherefore, we pray: entreat the Master of all that he enlighten your land with Orthodoxy in these latter times, and strengthen us therein.

Kontakion, Tone 1 - O martyrs of these latter times, ye whitened your garments in the blood of the Lamb, and shed your own blood for Christ. Wherefore, ye now minister unto him day and night in the Church of heaven. Therefore, entreat Christ for us, O glorious martyrs, that he preserve his little flock from the beguilement of the enemy, and that he lead us out of all tribulation unto a land of never-waning light.

Ikos - The armies of the angels rejoiced when ye fled from the darkness of paganism to the light of Orthodoxy, cleansing your souls and bodies of sins through holy baptism. And having accepted the heavy lot of serving Christ in this age of new paganism, we offer up before your icon such hymns as these: Rejoice, confessors of Christ amid this blasphemous age; rejoice, radiant stars of the East! Rejoice, faithful worshippers of the true God; rejoice, mighty contenders against the demons! Rejoice, beacons dispelling pagan darkness; rejoice, ye who trampled the vile idols underfoot! Rejoice, all-wondrous lilies of China; rejoice, ye who pray fervently for the enlightenment of your race! Rejoice, much-suffering sheep of the Shepherd who was slain for us; rejoice, towers of God-loving patience! Rejoice, fiery suns of divine love; rejoice, ye who from the night of ignorance attained unto the dawn of the knowledge of God! Rejoice, O glorious martyrs of China, who strengthen us to endure unto the end!

St. Jonah of Manchuria (October 7/20)

Troparion, Tone 4 – Thou wast a good pastor for the Russian people, who had departed in exodus to live in a foreign land, guiding them in every way, but especially by the love of Christ, in all ways providing a model of love unfeigned. O Father Jonah, holy hierarch of Christ, entreat him for the salvation of our souls.

Kontakion, Tone 3 – Thou didst not forbid the children to come to thee, O divinely blessed one, taking care for their daily needs, and establishing a safe haven for them. And even after thy repose thou hast not forsaken them; for in a dream thou didst heal a paralyzed boy. Wherefore, we cry out to thee: rejoice, O all-glorious wonderworker Jonah!

Ikos - Having acquired true and heartfelt love for God and neighbor, O holy hierarch, thou didst cry out to thy flock: "O children, love ye one another!" Thus wast thou a model for all in word and deed, in love, spirit, faith, and purity; wherefore, many wonders and signs of God's power were manifested in thee to the faithful. As thou standest now amid the incorporeal hosts of heaven, yet dost thou remain inseparable from thy children. O thou who communest with the saints, by thine intercessions guard us from all demonic assaults, and lift up to the heights of love the hearts of those who with thanksgiving cry unto thee: rejoice, O all-glorious wonderworker Jonah!

Prayer - O Blessed Jonah, wondrous ascetic and constant intercessor for us before God! Thou wast honored with the rank of bishop and didst show a wondrous love toward Christ, who strengthened thee in thy labors and podvigs by his grace. Thou didst serve thy flock and children, and therefore had great boldness on the earth before the All-Holy Trinity. When thou didst receive knowledge of thine imminent repose from the physician, thou didst hasten to the Lord with faith and humble prayer, accepting God's will, lamenting only about thy flock, and especially the children, entreating the Lord not to leave them orphaned. Now appealing to thy fervent intercession, we earnestly entreat thee: with the merciful eye of thy love look upon us sinners in need of thy help, strengthen the faithful in fervor, strengthen those who are fighting with their passions in ascetic labors, correct the slothful to struggle in pious zeal. Help all of us to love one another, as thou didst often admonish to keep this foremost commandment of Christ, and ask for us the visitation of the grace of the Holy Spirit. That keeping all thine instructions, we may be vouchsafed to inherit the kingdom of Christ and together with thee, glorify the Father, the Son, and the Holy Spirit unto the ages of ages. Amen.

St. John the Wonderworker of Shanghai (June 19/July 2)

Troparion, Tone 6 - Glorious apostle to an age of coldness and unbelief invested with the grace-filled power of the saints of old, divinely-illumined seer of heavenly mysteries, feeder of orphans, hope of the hopeless, thou didst enkindle on earth the fire of love for Christ upon the dark eve of the day of judgment; O holy hierarch John, pray now that this sacred flame may also rise from our hearts.

Kontakion, Tone 4 - Chosen wonderworker and superb servant of Christ who pourest out in the latter times inexhaustable streams of inspiration and multitudes of miracles. We pray thee with love and call out to thee: rejoice, O holy hierarch John, Wonderworker of the latter times.

Troparion, Tone 5 (Let us all praise and worship the Word) - Lo, Thy care for thy flock in its sojourn hath prefigured the supplications which thou dost ever offer up for the whole world. Thus do we believe, having come to know thy love, O holy hierarch and wonderworker John. Wholly sanctified by God through the ministry of the all-pure Mysteries and thyself ever strengthened thereby, thou didst hasten to the suffering, O most gladsome healer, wherefore speed now to the aid of us who honor thee with all our heart.

Kontakion, Tone 4 - Thy heart hath gone out to all who entreat thee with love, O holy hierarch John, and who remember the struggle of thy whole industrious life, and thy painless and easy repose, O faithful servant of the all-pure Directress.

Troparion, Tone 5 (Let us all praise and worship the Word) - Like a spiritual daystar in heaven's firmament thou didst encompass the whole world and didst enlighten men's souls, hence thy name is glorified in the east and the west, for thou shonest forth with the grace of the Sun of Righteousness, O John, our beloved shepherd. Wherefore, cease not to entreat Christ that he may have mercy on our souls.

Kontakion, Tone 8 (To thee the Champion Leader) - To thee the pastor and protector of a countless host of homeless orphans, paupers, and afflicted ones do we offer anthems born of love and thanksgiving. But as a hierarch filled with grace and zeal for piety, do thou save us from the foes of apostolic truth, for we cry to thee: rejoice, great wonderworker John!

Prayer - O beloved Hierarch John, while living amongst us thou didst see the future as if present, distant things as if near, and the hearts and minds of men as if they were thine own. We know that in this thou wast illumined by God, with whom thou wast ever in the mystical communion of prayer, and with whom thou now abidest eternally. As thou didst hear the mental petitions of thy far-scattered flock even before they could speak to thee, so now hear our prayers and bring them before the Lord. Thou hast gone over unto the life unaging, unto the other world, yet thou art in truth not far from us, for heaven is closer to us than our own souls. Show us who feel frightened and alone the same compassion that thou didst once show to the trembling fatherless ones. Give to us who have fallen into sin, confusion, and despair the same stern yet loving instruction that thou didst once give to thy chosen flock. In thee we see the living likeness of our Maker, the living spirit of the Gospel and the foundation of our faith. In the pure life that thou hast led during our sinful times, we see a model of virtue, a source of instruction and inspiration. Beholding the grace bestowed upon thee, we know that God hath not abandoned his people. It is rather we that have fallen from him, and so must regain the likeness of Divinity as thou hast done. Through thine intercession, O blessed one, grant that we may increase our striving toward our heavenly homeland, setting our affections on things above, laboring in prayer and virtue, waging war against the attacks of our fallen nature. Invoke the mercy of God, that we may one day join thee in his kingdom. For our deepest wish is to live forever with him, with the Father, and the Son and the Holy Spirit, now and ever and to the ages of ages. Amen.

St. Gury Archbishop of Tauris and Simferopol
(March 17/30)

Troparion, Tone 3 - O holy Father Gury with the Spirit of God hast thou enlightened the land of China by the light of the Gospel, thou hast conquered heresy and dissidence in the land of Tauris, spreading there the words of Christ, wherefore pray thou unto Christ for us who venerate thy healing relics, to grant divine grace and wisdom to our souls.

Kontakion, Tone 8 - Our godly wise mentor of meekness and humility, the glorious proponent of mercy and non-possessiveness, who dost enlighten thy faithful people with the light of the teachings of Christ, O Holy Father Gury, leave us not who honor thy memory.

Prayer - Our holy and glorious hierarch, O Father Gury, the glory of the town of Simferopol and the Crimean land! Abiding in vigils and fasting, thou didst marry thy soul to the Heavenly Bridegroom and become an abode of the All-Holy Trinity and now thou standest before Him together with the holy angels. Following St. Innocent of Irkutsk, thou didst bring new people to Christ and his Church from out of pagan darkness in the land of China, and didst strengthen them in the faith. Afterward in the blessed land of Tauris, thou didst labor untiringly, building churches and monasteries, giving a wise example of charity, gentleness, and love to all. O Holy Father Gury, look upon us thy children from before the all-holy and venerable throne of the Trinity, where thou dost boldly intercede for thy flock. With thy compassion, behold our infirmities, cure and comfort our distressed souls, ease the weight of our sins, and accept our prayer, which we offer with warm-hearted love to thee. Grant unto us thy children in the fatherland and in the diaspora that we may worthily labor on earth and maintain the Orthodox faith unshakable in our hearts unto the last day. Pray that, at the fearsome judgment seat of Christ, we may stand on the right hand of the Righteous Judge; and pray unceasingly for the salvation of our souls. Amen.

The Port Arthur Icon of the Most Holy Theotokos
(May 13/26 and August 16/29)

Troparion, in Tone 4 - Today, O Mother of God, the city of Vladivostok rejoices, and with it all the reaches of the earth, in beholding thine icon, which bears the historic name of Port Arthur, for blessed and glorious provision was offered to the devout forces of the far Russian realm, and is offered to us today as we gaze on thy holy image and cry, O Orthodox Christians of China, preserve the Orthodox faith, for this faith is your firm foundation.

Kontakion, Tone 8 (To thee the Champion Leader) - O Triumphant Lady, thy desire was to send thine icon to Port Arthur as victory for thy troops; and though this task was hindered by careless men, thy boundless love was not; for all who now praise thine icon with trust in thy prayer are anchored by hope in the port of heaven; thus we cry unto thee: rejoice, thou noetic ark of life!

Ikos - Come now, all who embrace wisdom, and let us console our Mother, who wraps us in the Comforter; for she is downcast at her children's rejection: for one dishonored her through want of faith, whilst another forgot her, being blinded by earthly cares; and all of us have forsaken her through our impenitence. But, let us now comprehend the worth of this treasure that lieth before us, and let us fervently venerate it, the all-wondrous icon of our Lady of Port Arthur; and she will carry us into the port of heaven, for she is the noetic ark of life!

Prayer – O Most Holy Virgin Theotokos, who art higher than the cherubim and the seraphim and art the holiest of all the saints, venerating thine icon we pray thee humbly: hearken to our prayers, thou who seest our sorrows and woes, and as our deeply loving mother be swift to assist us who are helpless. Entreat thy Son and our Lord that he not give our land over to our enemies and that he not deal with us as we deserve for our many iniquities, but rather may he grant us his abundant mercy as we turn from our sins. O our Lady, ask him in his goodness for the health of our bodies and the salvation of our souls, for a peaceful life and bountiful prosperity, for fair and seasonable weather, and a blessing upon our every good intention and undertaking. Thou didst mercifully give thine icon of Port Arthur in days past for the protection of Orthodox people, but the icon was held captive by the godless world because of faithlessness, unbelief, and rejection of that which is dear to Christ. And now we venerate thy recovered image, which is precious to us, and we offer to thee our zealous hymns and to thy Son our sincere repentance. O all-praised Queen, stretch forth thy God-bearing hands, with which thou didst carry the Christ Child, and pray that he deliver us from unbelief and every evil. Show us, O our Lady, the triumph of thy mercy: strengthen the faithful, enlighten those who have gone astray, heal the sick, comfort the afflicted, and help the poor. Protect our land beneath thy veil, gladden the people, fill the holy churches with those who are hungry to receive the Lord's goodness, enlighten all the nations of the world by the light of thy Son and our God, grant us to complete our earthly life in all piety and devotion, to have a good Christian end, and to inherit the heavenly kingdom by thy motherly intercession to Christ our Lord, begotten of thee. To him, with his eternal Father and Holy Spirit, be all glory, honor, and worship, now and ever and unto the ages of ages. Amen.

St. Innocent of Irkutsk
(November 26/December 9 and February 9/22)

Troparion, Tone 3 – O most radiant beacon of the Church, who hast illumined the Russian land with the rays of thy good works, and has glorified God by many healings of those who have recourse to thy reliquary with faith, O holy hierarch, our father, we entreat thee: protect thy city from all misfortune and grief.

Kontakion, Tone 4 – Ye faithful, let us all praise with love the pastor whose name signifieth innocence, the preacher of the faith among the pagans of Mongolia, the glory and adornment of the flock of Irkutsk; for he is the protector of this land and an intercessor for our souls.

Prayer – O saint of God, good pastor, faithful worker in the vineyard of Christ, hierarch and father, Innocent! Look down upon this city and its people, and pray to Christ our God to keep thy flock safe from the wolves that would destroy it: may he send down his Holy Spirit to make us walk wisely before him in all devotion and purity all the days of our life so that, glorifying his all-holy name day and night, we may be found worthy to be heirs also of life eternal, and may praise the name of the Father, and of the Son, and of the Holy Spirit, now and ever, and unto the ages of ages. Amen.

A hymn of praise to the Holy Martyrs of China who suffered under the Boxer Rebellion

The company of Chinese Orthodox martyrs—
The old and young, the parents and children,
The blind, the lame, and the poor—
Placed their hope in thee, O Jesus, and died for the sake of thy love, saying:
"We will not worship that which is unworthy of adoration—
Lifeless idols, the multitude of pagan gods that cannot save—
Nor will we deny him who was crucified for our sake
To receive from his enemies praise, peace, comfort, and an earthly life.
Rather, we count it an honor to die for him who died for us,
And like him, we offer ourselves as meek lambs for the slaughter.
You call us devils, but we worship Christ, the slayer of evil.
He is our strength and deliverer,
And having suffered with him,
We shall be glorified with him in his kingdom."

A hymn of praise to the Holy Hieromartyr Mitrophan of Beijing

Mitrophan the humble and peaceful priest of God
Patiently endured insults and forgave those who offended him.
He suffered the enmity of men and the malice of demons
With the grace of Christ, the prayers of the Mother of God,
And the help of the Cross, saying: "Who is weak, and I am not weak?
Who is made to fall, and I am not indignant?
But the grace of Jesus Christ is sufficient for me,
For his power is made perfect in weakness."
Under his roof, meek Mitrophan received those who were at enmity with him,
Blessing and encouraging them to be faithful to Christ.

The pagan mob, frenzied with demonic passions berated him, saying:
"You are Chinese. You must sacrifice to the Chinese gods."
But Mitrophan answered: "My God, Jesus Christ,
Is the God of the whole world and of all the nations.
From sin, corruption, and death he has saved all mankind."
Then, before him, the Boxers killed his wife and children.
"Now," they said, "how can you say your Jesus is so powerful?
He did not save them from death."
But Father Mitrophan replied, "No. He saved them.
They are not lost to me,
But I will see them in the heavenly kingdom."
"We see no heavenly kingdom," they said, jeering.
"You cannot see it because you are not baptized.
But if you truly believe in Jesus Christ,
He will open your eyes and show you the heavenly kingdom."
Then, the Boxers gouged out the eyes of blessed Mitrophan and said,
"Now, what do you see?"
"Now," replied God's worthy priest,
"I see the heavenly kingdom more clearly—
No longer with my bodily faculties,
But with the illumined eye of the heart."
The Boxers speared his chest like a honeycomb,
And the meek Father Mitrophan fell beneath a date tree.
Sweet is the memory of him who laid down his life
For his Friend, the God-Man, Jesus Christ,
Who bestows glory and honor upon his saints.

A hymn of praise to the Priest Stefan U, martyred by the Chinese Communists during the Cultural Revolution

The new martyr Stefan, the faithful priest of Madyagow,
Suffered for the love of Jesus Christ,
Bearing bodily the saving marks of the Savior's Passion.
He was mocked, humiliated, tortured, and spat upon,
But endured each blow and insult patiently, saying:
"The Lord is my helper. What can man do to me?
Who shall separate me from the love of Christ?"
In this way, Father Stefan defended the Orthodox faith
Even to the shedding of his blood.
His death is precious in the sight of the Lord,
Who has prepared imperishable crowns for those who love him,
Faithful unto death.

APPENDIX IV. THE HOLY MARTYRS OF CHINA[1]

(commemorated June 11/24)

Priest MITROPHAN, 45. He was known for humility and peacefulness, enduring insults with patience and never justifying himself. He considered his abilities and charity insufficient for the priesthood. Yet, after ordination, he served God tirelessly for 15 years, spending much time translating and editing books. Having suffered many insults from his own people and from unbelievers, he finally had a mild breakdown, which caused him to spend three years living outside the Mission, receiving only half of his previous salary. Despite this, he was known for his generosity, and many took advantage of him.

When the Boxer Rebellion broke out and the Mission was burned, many Orthodox Christians—including several who had previously despised him—took refuge in Fr. Mitrophan's home. He accepted them all and strengthened the distraught and fearful, telling them that now a time of trial had come upon them, and encouraging them to face it bravely.

Late on the evening of June 10, the house was surrounded by soldiers and Boxers. Around 70 Orthodox Christians were sheltered inside. Those who were able fled, but Fr. Mitrophan remained behind with the others—primarily woman and children—and faced torture and death together with them.

The Boxers punctured his chest like a honeycomb and he fell underneath a date tree in his courtyard. Several members of his family suffered with him, including his wife, Tatiana, and his sons, Isaiah and John.

TATIANA, 44. On June 10, she was initially saved from the Boxers by her daughter-in-law, Maria (Isaiah's wife), but on the following day, Tatiana was seized together with 19 others, sent to the Boxer camp, and beheaded.

ISAIAH, 23. He served in the artillery. On June 7, the Boxers, knowing he was a Christian, beheaded him.

JOHN (Ioann), 7. The Boxers displayed great cruelty in their treatment of this child in particular, splitting his shoulders and cutting off his

---

[1] From articles first published in Russian in the 1906 issue of *"Izvestia pravoslavnogo bratstva v Kitae,"* and then in the 1917 issue of *"Kitayskiy Blagovestnik"* (Chinese Good News). Recently republished in the 1/2000 issue of the revived Russian edition of *"Kitayskiy Blagovestnik."* This online edition was proofread against the accounts as published in the 1935 issue of *"Kitayskiy Blagovestnik."* The English translation is by Nina Tkachuk Dimas, 2004. The full account appears here: http://www.orthodox.cn/history/martyrs/1_en.htm. The version appearing in this appendix has been edited.

toes, in an attempt to make him renounce Christ. His sister-in-law Maria saved him from death, hiding him in a latrine. On the morning of June 11, he was found sitting at the entrance of the house, without clothes or shoes. People asked, "Are you hurting?" He answered, "It doesn't hurt." Boys scoffed at him, calling him a devil, but he answered, "I believe in God, and am not a devil." The pagans called Christians devils and devil's disciples. John asked neighbors for water, but they chased him away. Protasy Chang and Irodion Xu, who were not yet baptized, testified that they saw John's wounds were 1¾ inches deep, but he felt no pain and, when seized again by the Boxers, he felt no fear and went peacefully. One old man expressed regret about him, saying, "What is this boy guilty of? It is his parents' fault that he became a devil's disciple." Others made fun of him, deriding him and smiling contemptuously. Imitating the Lord Jesus Christ, the young martyr was taken as a lamb to slaughter.

MARIA, 19, wife of Fr. Mitrophan's son, Isaiah. Two days before the Boxers' pogrom, she came to Fr. Mitrophan's home, wishing to die in her groom's family. When the Boxers surrounded Fr. Mitrophan's house, she courageously rescued others, helping them over the walls. When the Boxers broke down the doors and entered the courtyard, Maria bravely accused them of lawlessness, and they did not dare to kill her, but simply wounded her hand and pierced her leg. She exhibited uncommon courage. Fr. Mitrophan's son, Sergei, three times tried to convince her to leave and hide, but she answered: "I was born near the church of the Most Holy Mother of God and here I will die." Soon more Boxers arrived and this courageous woman was martyred, considering death as departure to a place of blessed rest.

PAUL (Pavel) Wang Wenheng, 36. Before turning 20, he was appointed to the post of catechist, since he was honest, obedient, submissive, and a gifted communicator. He was particularly like-minded with Fr. Mitrophan. On June 2, his property was plundered and his house was destroyed. Having taken what silver could be rescued, he sought safety with pagan relatives. But with guile, first they took him in, then they took his silver, and then they chased him away. He was hard-working, thrifty, and kind, but during the days of disaster, he had no food. He was martyred on the evening of June 10. Suffering the same fate together with him were his mother **Ekaterina**, 62; wife **Sarah**, 37; son **Ioann**, 11; and daughter **Alexandra**, 9. Before dying, Paul prayed to God kneeling with arms crossed on his chest. Before Ekaterina's martyrdom, she, having poor eyesight, wandered around the city hiding from the Boxers; she was accused of being a well-poisoner, stripped, and pushed into a bog.

JOACHIM, 19, nephew of Paul, was seized by the Boxers on June 4 and killed near the northeast tower of the city wall.

INNOKENTY (Innocent) Fang Zhihai, 48. He was baptized in infancy. He sang well and for a long time was the Mission school teacher. He was an honest and sincere person. Archimandrite Innokenty (Figurovsky) greatly appreciated him, appointed him economos [housekeeping manager], and was preparing him for ordination to the diaconate. He was martyred with his wife **Elena**, 49, and their children: the elder son, **Evmeny**, 17; the daughters **Sophia**, 9; and **Nadezhda (Hope)**, 9. On June 1, when the Boxers burned the church, Innokenty's house was also plundered and burned. The next day, Innokenty hid in Fr. Mitrophan's house, while his wife with two daughters hid with relatives, but on the evening of June 2, these betrayed them to the Boxers. The Boxers returned the girls, but Elena was taken to a pagan temple where attempts were made to have her bow before idols, but she strenuously resisted. After this, she was made to kneel in the street and twice struck on the neck with a dagger. She lost consciousness and the Boxers, considering her dead, ordered the guard to put her aside. By morning, Elena regained consciousness. Noticing this, a guard freed her from the matting in which she was wrapped, brushed the soil off her, and released her. Christians, hearing what happened to Elena, led her to the house of Fr. Mitrophan. Seeing Elena stained with blood and hearing her story, how she suffered for Christ, all began to cry and expressed the hope that the Lord would preserve her life. But, as she began to recover from her wounds, on June 10 she died a martyr's death with the others. That day, June 10, Innokenty, fleeing the Boxers through the courtyard wall, injured his face. On the morning of the next day, he sat at the Mission site well, holding his daughter Nadezhda on his lap. This girl was rescued from a fire, her hair was singed, her white shirt was dirtied with blood -- probably she was wounded by the Boxers. Fr. Mitrophan's son Sergei twice tried to convince Innokenty to hide. But he replied: "I and my daughter are wounded; it is difficult for us to hide; it is better to die near the church." Soon Boxers arrived. Innokenty, it is said, jumped into the well -- which had little water -- and the Boxers stoned him. When this well was dug up in 1903, four whole corpses were found there. They were buried under the altar of the Church of the Martyrs.

On the morning of the 10th, before the attack on the Christians in Fr. Mitrophan's house, Innokenty's elder son Evmeny was taken to a military post. It is unknown where he died. Innokenty's daughter Sophia probably burned in Fr. Mitrophan's house, together with more than 10 other girls.

An Albazinian, **KLIMENT (Clement)**, Kui Ling, 36. He suffered with his wife **Barbara**, 35, and their children: **Maria**, 14; **Olga**, 11; **Ia**, 9; and **Irina**, 4. The day that the Mission buildings were burned, Kliment and his family hid in their family cemetery outside the city. Later, they were executed together with others on June 11. Kliment was a sacristan since his youth and served very assiduously. His mother, **Ia**, 56, and a widow from a young age, was the principal of the Mission's school for females, and was in charge of handicrafts for church decoration. She died a martyr's death in Fr. Mitrophan's home on June 10. The Boxers chopped off her leg before her death.

MATTHEW Hai Qun, 31, assistant to the sacristan, suffered with his wife, **Matrona**, 32. On June 11, at about 7 o'clock in the morning, Matthew and Matrona with their daughter **Agafia**, 5, fled toward the Mission, pursued by a soldier with a dagger in his hand. At that time, the Mission was filled with Boxers. Matthew, Matrona, and Agafia were seized and executed.

VITUS Hai, Matthew's brother, 29. On June 11, he was killed in the Cheng'ensi pagan temple and burned. Vitus read well in Slavonic. His wife **Martha**, whom he had recently married, was martyred with him, together with Matthew's second brother, **Nikifor** Hai, 27, sisters **Vassa** Zhong, 25, and **Elena** Zhong, 19, third brother, **Kirill** Hai, 15, their mother, **Ekaterina** Zhun, 55 and a widow, their grandmother **Nadezhda** Chang, 81 and a widow, and their uncle, **Alexei** Ming, 51. Their cousin, **Boniface**, 25, and his son, **Taisii**, were also killed. Vitus' younger brother, **Stefan**, 19, was taken by the Boxers into slavery, and then killed.

An Albazinian, **SIMEON** Xi Lin'a, 50, formerly a sacristan and bell ringer, had lately been baking prosphora (church bread). On June 10, he was among those surrounded by the Boxers and killed, probably in the Cheng'ensi pagan temple.

Albazinian maidens, **EKATERINA**, 24, and **MUZA (Muse)**, 17, died as martyrs in the house of Vitt Hai, which later became the site of a women's monastery. They tried to flee from the burning house over a wall, but the Boxers pierced them with spears and threw them down into the courtyard of the burning house.

MARINA Xu, 44, widowed for many years, was a teacher at the Mission's school for females. On June 2, Marina, together with her brother Kassian Lin's wife, Liudmila, and her children: Vladimir, Nikita and Georgy, went to Alexander Cheng's house. She said that she fled only for the sake of the children, and had she been alone, she would have sacrificed herself to God when the church burned. Alexander's wife's brother was afraid to let Marina and Liudmila with the children into the house. Khrisanf In, who was there also said it was dangerous for Christians to gather in one place. Therefore,

Marina and Liudmila, after washing up and drinking tea, returned to Shizijie (near the Mission) and lived there until June 10. When on the evening of June 10 the Boxers began attacking the Christians, Marina and Liudmila hid within the house concealed by darkness. Passing near that house, the Boxers opened a rear window, looked and threw a torch inside the house, but did not notice Maria and Liudmila with her children. At the time, they were kneeling and praying. On June 11, Marina separated from Liudmila and went to her husband's relatives in the southeast part of the city, but there she was seized by the Boxers and killed. And Liudmila, with her children, after wandering about the city as beggars, were finally able to get out of the city and were saved. Liudmila's son, Vladimir, went on to serve as a deacon.

An Albazinian, **ANNA** Rui, 57, a widow. Her **two married daughters** are among those who died as martyrs; a third daughter, later the nun Fiva, and son, later the priest Mikhail Min, had been in the hands of the Boxers, but were saved. Anna herself died on the evening of June 10. When the Boxers broke into the house, Anna strongly reproached them. Grown furious, the Boxers chopped her with swords and later burned her body completely.

PETER Li Yongan, 27, chorister, conducted meteorological observations. On June 2, Peter's house was plundered. His was a large family living together, primarily women and children. Having lost this shelter, they hid in Fr. Mitrophan's house and in other places. Peter was killed by the Boxers on June 10 in the house of Michael Wen. His corpse was seen pressed down by a thrown beam. Peter's wife, **Evfimia**, 22, and daughter, **Artemia**, 4, also died as martyrs His son, **Filimon**, a 1-year-old infant, the Boxers threw onto the road. **Maria**, 37, the wife of Peter's elder brother Matthew Li, with several children, among whom was Fr. Mitrophan's son, Ioann, hid in her mother's home, but the local residents drove them out. Later, the Boxers seized them and wanted to boil them in a cauldron, but at the time, the government's protection of the Boxers had not yet been announced, and they did not dare kill Christians; moreover, many good people expressed compassion for the children; therefore the Boxers released Maria with the children. On June 10, she was among those who were surrounded by the Boxers near the Mission site. On the morning of the 11th, Fr. Mitrophan's son Sergei saw her at the Mission site near the well under a tree and tried to convince her to hide, but she showed no fear and calmly spoke to Innokenty Fang. It was here that she accepted a martyr's death. Her body was later found in the well with Innokenty's body -- it is not known whether she was killed with stones in the well or thrown there after being killed. Maria's two daughters, **Anisia**, 14, and **Melania**, 3, were likely burned in Father Mitrophan's house.

An Albazinian, **ALEXANDRA** Li, 32, widow, sister of the catechist Paul. Alexandra had esteemed her deceased husband Evmeny, who had helped Archimandrite Flavian with translations and was the brother of Peter Li, as Sarah had esteemed Abraham. On the evening of June 10, she was among those surrounded by the Boxers in Fr. Mitrophan's house and did not want to seek safety in flight. When the Boxers broke down a door, she was probably one of the first to be killed. The Boxers burned her with torches, so that her whole body broke apart. Her body lay to the right side of Fr. Mitrophan's body. Alexandra's two daughters, **Artemia**, 15, and **Evdokia**, 12, were probably also burned to death in Fr. Mitrophan's house.

An Albazinian, **ALEXEY** Ying, 27, a chorister from early childhood. On June 10, Alexey avoided death, but then several days later returned to his acquaintance, Zhun, in order to borrow money. A neighbor seized him, put a cord around his neck, and lead him to the pagan temple of Cheng'ensi, where Alexey endured a martyr's death. His mother, **Susanna** A, 59, a widow, was martyred on June 11. It is not known where Alexey's older brother, **David**, 37, died. His other older brother, **Evfimy**, 35, and lame, on June 11 was walking by the southwest corner of the Mission. There a certain Yu Sang began to berate him for being a Christian. Evfimy answered with sharp words. Then, having run into his house, Yu Sang jumped out with a dagger and struck Evfimy many times. Evfimy fell to the ground, but soon regained consciousness and headed for his own house. Yu Sang, learning that Evfimy had not died, went after him with many others and at first pelted him with stones, and later killed him at a place named Wuyueguan. This Boxer, Yu Sang, remained alive after the war, but he incurred a heavy punishment: he lost use of the lower part of his body so that he could not move at all.

AFANASY (Athanasius) Yu, 21, studied in the Mission school from an early age and was a chorister. In May, when the public disturbances began, he went to Dōngdìngān together with Archimandrite Innokenty. Having calmed the Christians, Fr. Innokenty returned to Peking, but Afanasy remained in Dōngdìngān with Fr. Mitrophan's son Sergei who lived there at the church. On the evening of May 25 the Dōngdìngān church was burned by the Boxers, and Afanasy with Sergei fled to Peking. Then on June 10, Afanasy endured a martyr's death in his father's house. Others who died there in addition to Afanasy: his grandmother **Olga** A, 75 and a widow; his aunt, **Agafia** He, 50, Olga's daughter; his father, **Sergy** Shuan, 47, Olga's son; his mother **Anna**, 40; his brothers: **Pavel**, 17; **Evgeny**, 8; and **Kir**, 4. His sister was Maria, the bride of Fr. Mitrophan's son Isaiah, who died at the Mission.

An Albazinian, **AFANASY** Ah, 58-59. He studied at the Mission school since a young age. At around age 16, he fell from a city wall and from then on was a cripple: his legs were withered and he moved with the help of his hands. Afanasy hid from the Boxers in the empty, broken down buildings of Siyefu. On the evening of June 11, a Boxer threatened him with a spear and drove him out to Beiguanyu. Afanasy was then seized with other Christians, but because he could not walk quickly, the Boxers killed him in the same place where he was seized, and then burned his body. Protasy Chan testified to this as he was an eyewitness. He said Afanasy accepted death silently. Afanasy's wife **Varvara**, 45, and their children: **Pelagia**, 17; **Maria**, 9; **Savva**, 6, probably died at the Mission on June 11.

An Albazinian, **MYRON** Rui, 49, his wife **Maria**, 43, and their children: **Martha**, 21; **Anastasia**, 19; **Eudoxia**, 16; **Innokenty**, 14 ; **Savva**, 12; **Nil**, 10; **Maria**, 7; **Elena**, 4. They accepted martyrdom in their apartment near the Mission on June 10. However, it is known that, having been wounded by the Boxers, Myron did not die, but could not move. On the morning of June 11, at about 6 o'clock, neighbors continued hitting him with bricks, then the Boxers arrived and killed him. At this time, Fr. Mitrophan's son Sergei came to the Mission site for the last time and heard Myron's dying cries.

LYUBOV Chang, 22, a maiden. She studied at the Mission school since childhood, and later taught and lived there. When the Mission buildings were burned, she hid in the house of Fr. Mitrophan. Having been saved from Fr. Mitrophan's house when Christians were being slaughtered (June 10), Lyubov with her brother Ioasaph and another elderly widow, **Anna Se**, 67, hid in the house of someone named Song, who was subsequently baptized. Here Lyubov and Anna, hiding in a closet, were turned over to the Boxers and killed. It is not known where Lyubov's mother, **Maria** Chang, 65, died. Lyubov's niece **Sira**, 6, who was Joseph's daughter, burned to death in Fr. Mitrophan's house. On June 11, Lyubov's brother **Joseph** Rong, 37, was again near the Mission and, being surrounded from all directions by the approaching Boxers, ran into Fr. Mitrophan's courtyard and hanged himself on a belt. According to to one soldier, the Boxers pursuing Joseph beheaded him right after he hanged himself on a tree.

DOROTHEA, wife of Tikhon Wu, 43. In early childhood she studied at the Mission school. She was martyred on June 10 in Fr. Mitrophan's house. Dying together with her were her son **Mina**, 12, and her widowed mother **Anastasia** Li, 63.

KAPITON Ying-yuan, 43, his wife, **Paraskeva**, 40. They were martyred during the night of June 10 as they attempted to flee. Kapiton had been a chorister and was engaged in copying music.

VICTOR Fu, 48, baptized as an adult. He was a servant at the Mission's school for males. His wife **Marina**, 29, studied at the Mission's school for females. They were martyred with their children: **Herman**, 10; **Faith**, 8; **Mathew**, 3; and an adopted daughter, **Hope**, 16. On June 11, the Boxers, did a house-to-house search for Christians and missed Victor's house, but a neighbor named You betrayed them to the Boxers and they were martyred. Before dying, Victor spoke to the Boxers: "Violent ruiners! Of what are we guilty?" The Boxers assaulted him and did not spare the children. Having killed Victor, they took out his heart and offered it as a sacrifice.

PETER Wang, 51, was a humble man. On June 11 he, together with his wife, **Anisia**, 44, and son, **John** Song, 14, were seized by the Boxers and executed. Martyred together with them were: **Aquilina**, 33, and wife of Peter's deceased brother, and her children: **Sergei**, 13; **Anania**, 11; and **Pelagia**, 5. Peter also had a daughter **Elena**, 20, from his first wife; she was martyred also.

PHILLIP Antoniev Li Ruixing, 45; his wife, **Anna**, 37, and son **Thomas**, 7, lived at the Russian embassy, where Phillip was the senior servant. When the embassies were besieged, Phillip fled from the city with his family and his relatives beyond the southwest gate. But local residents, learning that they were Christians, betrayed them to be tortured and killed.

ALEXEY Hang Wenheng, 42, his wife **Thecla**, 34, their children: **Theoktist**, 14; **Anna**, 12; **Iulita**, 7; **Sofonia**, 5; and **Nicholas**, 1. On June 11, not having the opportunity to hide from the Boxers, they -- on someone's advice -- poisoned themselves with opium. But when they were still alive, the Boxers arrived and manifested their barbarity by removing Alexey's heart and biting it.

THEODORE Yue, 60, his wife **Elizabeth**, 51. On June 10, when the Mission buildings were burned, Theodore and Elizabeth hid in the house of their son-in-law, Alexey Hang. It is not known whether they died in Alexey's house or elsewhere. Theodore's daughter, **Tatiana**, 18, had married a pagan. During the Boxer Rebellion, her mother-in-law caused her much suffering; she fell ill and died, but others say she was killed.

ELIAS Quan, 32, his wife **Elena**, 26, and their children: **John**, 2; and a **newborn son**. On June 11, neighbors betrayed them to the Boxers. Elias' newborn son the Boxers cut in half with an axe. Elias' brother, **Gerasim**, 25, secured his life for a big sum of money, but before Peking was taken by foreign armies, the Boxers killed him, fearing revenge.

MINODORA Wang, 59, her older son **Andrew**, 35, and his wife **Anna**, 29, and their daughter **Sophia**, 5; Minodora's second son **John**, 33, and his wife **Daria**, 22, and their son **Theodosius**, 5; **Maria**, 23, wife of Minodora's third son, **David**, their son **Mark**, 3, and **an unborn child**. They were all martyred on the evening of June 10 in the Vitus Hai home. Maria was pregnant at the time.

SERGEI Filippov Zhang, 49, a widower, who studied at the Mission school in early childhood. He knew Russian and was a chorister all his life. He was probably martyred together with his son **John**, 19, on June 10, at his home.

An Albazinian, **ALEXANDER** Heng Gui, 33, a merchant. On June 6, he was betrayed to the Boxers and killed.

LEV Hai Ling, 39, together with his father, **Savva** Tsin, 61, and son **John**, 14. The place and manner of their death are unknown.

SAMPSON Nikolaev Pan, 36, his wife **Anna**, 32, and their son **Evdokim**, 7. On June 15, the Boxers severed Sampson's head and carried it through the street on a club shouting: "This is Sampson's head."

An Albazinian, **PAUL** Sang, 60, the brother of Monk Papiy.

DANIEL De, 30, his father **Trofim** Gong, 53, and mother **Ekaterina**, 52.

GEORGE Lian Xi, 42.

ANNA Lin, 81, a widow from among the wards of the Mission.

MATRONA Lian, 46. When the Mission was destroyed, Matrona with her younger daughter **Mavra**, 10, was evicted from her apartment by the pagan landlord and hid in Fr. Mitrophan's house. She and her daughter Mavra died there. Matrona's **older daughter** -- her name is forgotten -- had married a pagan, and when the Boxer uprising began, her husband's relatives starved her to death.

EVFIMY Pan, 42, was stoned in the street on June 11. His wife **Fevronia**, 36, was probably burned in the house.

AKILINA Shuang, 25; her widowed mother-in-law **Anna** Chang, 61; her husband **Paul** Konstantinov Shuang, 39; and children: **Ioann**, 10;

Makrina, 4; and **Ioann**, 2. Neighbors promised to conceal them, but instead betrayed them and their house was set on fire, beginning with the windows and doors, so that all those inside perished in the fire.

IRINA Gui Ruishi, 54, and her husband **Ionah** Gui, 61. Irina was a woman of modest outlook, who attended church daily. When she was pointed out as a "devil" to Boxers searching for Christians, she, in simplicity of heart, answered: "We are not 'devils,' but Christians."

An Albazinian, **IRINA** Fu, 35. Irina's children: **Anna**, 17; **Athanasia**, 10; **Evpraksiya**, 8; **Prokhor**, 6; **Natria**, 3. Irina's sister-in-law **Pelagia**, 44, died together with her and the children.

ANNA Bai, widow, 62. She lived in the Mission almshouse with her son, **Antoni**, 16.

ZOYA Shuang, about 45, widow. She, together with her daughter **Alexandra**, 11, and her son **Andrei**, 7, lived at the Mission almshouse.

An Albazinian, **KAPITOLINA** Huai, widow, 62. After her husband's death, being in great poverty and forced by her son-in-law, she renounced the faith. After this, she lost the use of her legs. Shortly before the Boxer Rebellion, Kapitolina repented of her apostasy and probably died beyond the Āndingmén Gate.

An Albazinian, **AGAFIYA** Rui, widow, 55. She lived at the Mission almshouse.

AKILINA Guang, widow, 47. She lived at the Mission almshouse. Her children were **Evstolia**, 14, and **Kifa**, 11. They probably died on June 10, when the Christians were attacked. It is not known where.

EVGENI Vasilevich Ji, 47, Manchurian soldier, was martyred on June 7 and thrown down a well.

An Albazinian **EVFIMIA**, 12, was martyred on June 10, in Fr. Mitrophan's house.

An Albazinian, **FEODOT** Gordiev Rui, 60, was martyred in his house near the Mission, on June 10.

MIKHAIL Quan, with his **wife** and **three children**, were seized and killed by the Boxers on June 8.

MARIA Chen, 3, died of illness while in Boxer captivity.

ELENA Quan, 6, died of illness while in Boxer captivity.

SIMEON Zhun; his niece, **Maria** Zhun, 5; her sister, **Nina**, 8; and her brother, **Vasili**, 3, died of illness while in Boxer captivity.

ELENA Huo, widow, 73; **Olimpiada** Jin, widow 61; and Olimpiada's daughter **Olga**, 19, suffered martyrdom on June 10 near the Mission.

FEVRONIA Fu, 72, was killed on June 1.

ANNA Li, widow, 58.

NIKON Huo, 23.

ANDREI Zhu Ling, 54, suffered on June 10 at the Mission site.

PETR Chang, 57, endured martyrdom on June 11.

IONA, adopted son of Alexei Hang Wenheng, 19.

DARIA De, 54, widow, and her granddaughter **Agafia**, endured martyrdom, on June 11.

An Albazinian, **PAVEL** Nikolaevich Dong, 48; his wife **Evgenia** Mihailovna, 38, and their children: **Iuliania**, 13; **Lukia**, 9; **Stefan**, 7, endured martyrdom on June 20.

DARIA, 33, sister of Nikolai Ji, endured martyrdom on June 23.

ISAIAH Se, 62, a Manchurian, died June 22 beyond the Dongzhímén Gate.

ANNA, 56, wife of the Albazinian, Georgy Ah, and **Anna**, 36, Gregory's daughter, were martyred near Shiyiyuan.

An Albazinian, **NIKOLAI**, 22.

Orthodox Christians slaughtered in the village of Dōngdìngān:

ALEXEI Zhang, 48, church caretaker; his wife **Evfimia**, 44; and children: **Evdokia**, 11; **Nikita**, 10, **Michael**, 6; **Maria**, 1.

STEFAN Wang Yuguang, 61.

KIR Zhin Fucheng, 60. His son, **John**, was sick with fever and was killed by the Boxers together with his father. His son Basil's **wife** with their **three children** fled to Baizhuāng after the church was burned and hid in a bog. They were killed there the next day and, though not yet baptized, they can be considered as having been baptized by fire.

IRINA, 55. She was only recently baptized at a time when the Boxers were starting to persecute Christians, and many rebuked her for being baptized. Later she was killed by the Boxers near the village of Dōngdìngān.

BIBLIOGRAPHY

1. Aleksandrov B.G. Bei-Guan. Brief History of the Russian Ecclesiastical Mission in China. Moscow, Saint Petersburg, 2006.
2. Gan Serafim, Deacon. Short biography of St Jonah of Hankou. http://www.orthodox.cn/saints/jonahpokrovsky/life_stjonaen.htm
3. Damascene (Christensen), Hieromonk. Christ, the Eternal Tao. Kitaysky Blagovestnik (Chinese Good News Messenger). Moscow, 1999, #2.
4. Datsyshen, V.G. Bishop Innokenty (Figurovsky). Beginning of a New Period in a History of the Russian Ecclesiastical Mission in Beijing. / Kitaysky blagovestnik (Chinese Good News Messenger). - Moscow, 2000, #1.
5. Datsyshen, V.G. Study of the Chinese Language in Russia (the 18th c. - the beginning of the 20th c.). - Novosibirsk, 2011.
6. Datsyshen, V.G. History of the Russian Ecclesiastical Mission in China. - Hong Kong, 2010.
7. Datsyshen, V.G. The Chinese in Siberia in the 17th c. - the 20th c.: problems of migrations and adaptations. - Krasnoyarsk, 2008.
8. Datsyshen, V.G. Metropolitan Innokenty of Beijing. - Hong Kong, 2011.
9. Datsyshen, V.G. "The Mystery of Peter (Kamensky) and Russian Sinology." http://www.synologia.ru/
10. Datsyshen, V.G. Christianity in China: The History and the Present. - Moscow, 2007.
11. The Tree. Orthodox Encyclopedia. http://drevo-info.ru/articles/22695.html
12. Archpriest Johan Du. Development of Russian Orthodox Church in Tianjin and its Environs. / Kitaysky Blagovestnik (Chinese Good News Messenger). - Moscow, 1999, #2.
13. Dyakov, I. About the Experience in Manchuria for the Faith and the Motherland. - Moscow, 2000.
14. Zhilevich, T. In Memory of the Dead in the Land of Manchuria and Harbintsah. - Melbourne, 2000.
15. Forgotten Temples of Harbin. http://religion.ng.ru/style/2006-08-16/8_hramy.html
16. Zavyalova, O. The Chinese Language in Russia: from Father Iakinf to the Internet. Russian Academy of Sciences, Institute of Far Eastern Studies. http://www.abirus.ru/content/564/623/625/643/823.html

17. Ivanov, P. Priest. Orthodox Translations of the New Testament in Chinese.
    http://www.orthodox.cn/localchurch/199803pivanov_ru.htm
18. Ipatova, A.S. The Russian Ecclesiastical Mission in China: The 20th century. / History of the Russian Ecclesiastical Mission in China. - Moscow, 1997.
19. Kamchatka Diocesan Gazette, 1894. - Blagoveshchensk, 1894.
20. Kamchatka Diocesan Gazette, 1895. - Blagoveshchensk, 1895.
21. Karyagin, K.M. Confucius. His Life and Philosophical Activity. / Buddha. Confucius. Mahomet. Saint Francis of Assisi. Savonarola: Biographical Sketches. - Moscow, 1995.
22. Kirillov, A. An Episode from the Life of the Russian Ecclesiastical Mission in China. / Kitaysky blagovestnik (Chinese Good News Messenger). - Moscow, 1999, #2.
23. Kradin, N. Russian Atlantis. - Khabarovsk, 2010.
24. Lomanov, A.V. Christianity and Chinese Culture. - Moscow, 2002.
25. Makoveychuk, Yu. Mikhail Drozdov: Our Man in Shanghai. 2012.
    http://www.pravmir.ru/mixail-drozdov-nash-chelovek-v-shanxae/
26. Manakova, T.B. The Red Fanza of the Russian Federation Embassy in Beijing. Beijing. - Moscow, 2007.
27. Manchurian Wedge. (Under the general editorship of Zabiyako, A.P.). - Blagoveshchensk, 2005.
28. Nikolai (Adoratsky), Hieromonk. The History of the Beijing Ecclesiastical Mission in the First Period of its Activity (1685 - 1745). / History of the Russian Ecclesiastical Mission in China. - Moscow, 1997.
29. Pozdnyaev, Dionisy Archpriest. At the Interfaces Between Paganism, Globalisation and Spiritual Thirst. / "Foma" Magazine, #3 (119), March 2003.
30. Pozdnyaev, Dionisy Priest. Orthodoxy in China (1900 - 1997). - Moscow,1998.
    http://www.orthodox.cn/localchurch/pozdnyaev/index_ru.html
31. Pozdnyaev, Dionisy Archpriest. Orthodoxy in China is the Issue that Must be Raised to the All-Church Level. / Interfax - Religion.2010.
    http://www.interfaxreligion.ru/orthodoxy/?act=interview&div=2 84&domain=1
32. Pozdnyaev, Dionisy Archpriest. Orthodox Consciousness and Chinese World: from a Conflict to a Dialogue.
    http://www.orthodox.cn/contemporary/hongkong/hbr_ru.htm
33. Pozdnyaev, Dionisy Priest. Chinese Holy Martyrs. - Moscow, 2000.
34. Orthodoxy in China. / Under the editorship of M.L.Titarenko. - Moscow, 2010.

35. Samoylov, N.A. Sino-Russian Treaties of 1858 and the Activities of the Amur Ecclesiastical Mission. / Orthodoxy in the Far East. - St. Petersburg, 2001, vol. 3.

36. Seraphim (Rose), Hieromonk. The Soul of China. / Kitaysky Blagovestnik (Chinese Messenger). - Moscow, 2000, #1.

37. Tikhvinsky, S.L.; Peskova, G.N. Prominent Russian Sinologist Father Ioakinf (Bichurin). / History of Russian Ecclesiastical Mission in China. - Moscow, 1997.

38. Tokmakova, A. Jonah, Bishop of Hankou. / Amurskaya Pravda. 24.06.2006.

39. Fuganov, A.S. To the Anniversary of the Beijing Ecclesiastical Mission and its Destroyed Church. / The Bulletin of the Russian Christian Humanitarian Academy. - Saint Petersburg, 2013, vol. 14, issue 1, pp. 34 - 40.

40. Ching (or Zin), Julia. Love of the New Testament, Humanity of Confucius and Fight in the Chinese Christianity of the 20th Century. / Kitaysky Blagovestnik (Chinese Good News Messenger). - Moscow, 2000, #1.

41. People's Republic of China. Operation World. http://www.operationworld.org/chna April 2013.

42. 东正教和东正教在中国 / 张绥著. 第1版. 上海：學林出版社：新華書店上海发行所发行, 1986. Translated by Anna L. Limanskaya.

ABOUT THE EXHIBIT "ORTHODOXY IN CHINA"

The materials from the exhibit "Orthodoxy in China" were displayed in Blagoveshchensk in 2013, coinciding with Patriarch Kirill's visit to China from May 10-15, 2013. A delegation of an Orthodox Chinese from Harbin and Beijing and Father Dionisy Pozdnyaev from Hong Kong attended the opening.

Made in the USA
Middletown, DE
23 May 2015